MA

MALVERN

Shih Tzu

TAMMY GAGNE

Shih Tzu
An Interpet Book

Project Team
Editor: Heather Russell-Revesz
Copy Editor: Ellen Fusz
Series Design: Leah Lococo, Ltd and Stephanie Krautheim
Design: Angela Stanford

First Published in UK by
Interpet Publishing
Vincent Lane
Dorking
Surrey
RH4 3YX

ISBN: 978 1 84286 160 8

Printed and bound in China

This book has been published with the intent to provide accurate and authoritative information in regard to the subject matter within. While every precaution has been taken in preparation of this book, the author and publisher expressly disclaim responsibility for any errors, omissions, or adverse effects arising from the use or application of the information contained herein. The techniques and suggestions are used at the reader's discretion and are not to be considered a substitute for veterinary care. If you suspect a medical problem consult your veterinarian.

www.interpet.co.uk

Table of Contents

Chapter 1

Why I Adore My
Shih Tzu

The name Shih Tzu means "little lion" in Chinese.
To those who know the breed best, this is not
surprising. These diminutive dogs are often
compared to the most admired of the large cats.
Similar to the lion, the Shih Tzu has an
all-knowing appearance that suggests he grasps
something very profound that eludes most humans.
Unlike his namesake, however,
the Shih Tzu is also known for his
sociable temperament.

S hih Tzu are frequently described as being friendly to a fault, a fitting trait for a dog bred first and foremost to be a companion.

Shih Tzu Origins

Originating in Tibet, Shih Tzu (pronounced 'shi zoo', with a silent 'h; and 'shi' as in 'ship') were first brought to China during the seventeenth century. Both countries considered the breed to be sacred animals; most were kept in temples or owned by royalty. The China Kennel Club, established in Shanghai in 1923, was probably the first such group to formally acknowledge the breed. By the time the Peking Kennel Club was formed in 1934, though, great confusion arose as to the differences between some of the smaller breeds there. While some people insisted that the Shih Tzu was a pure breed, others claimed that it was instead a cross between the Tibetan Apso and the Pekingese. Because of all the uncertainty, the Shih Tzu wasn't granted individual breed status from this organisation until 1938. In England, however, where the breed had been introduced in 1920, the Shih Tzu was recognised as a breed in 1933.

The communist takeover of Peking in 1949 led to a ban on the export of the Shih Tzu breed. Due to the small numbers of breeding pairs outside

China at this time, Pekingese dogs were then indeed crossed with the English line when breeders there began to fear the development of poor structure. Although the initial goal of strengthening the breed by shortening it was indeed accomplished, the unforeseen effect of bowed legs also resulted from this cross. This problem is still occasionally seen in the Shih Tzu breed today.

In the UK

In the 1930s the breed was first brought to Britain, and was recognised by the Kennel Club (KC) in 1940. In the UK, the Shih Tzu is a member of the utility group, in the US Toy group. Commonly referred to as "the chrysanthemum-faced dog" because of the breed's trademark hair that grows in all directions, the Shih Tzu has risen to great popularity in the both the UK and the US.

What Should A Shih Tzu Look Like?

During the breed's development in England, fanciers overwhelmingly decided that a smaller sized Shih Tzu best represented the dog's heritage, so Britain's Kennel Club (KC) established an ideal weight standard of 9 to 16

pounds (4 to 7 kg) at this time. The AKC later adopted this standard as well. Additionally, the standard states that an ideal Shih Tzu's body should measure

SENIOR DOG TIP

Good News on Ageing

If you're like me, you grew up hearing (and perhaps even believing) that old cliché about a year being equivalent to seven *dog years*. More recently it has been noted that this conversion method simply isn't reliable—particularly in the case of smaller breeds that often outlive larger dogs. Your Shih Tzu will reach adulthood quickly; by the time he is two years old, for instance, his age will be more comparable to a 20-year-old than 14-year-old. After that, though, a more logical formula for determining your dog's human age would be considering each additional year to be the equivalent of 4 human years. So your 10-year-old Shih Tzu who you thought was a senior citizen is actually just a seasoned adult. With a potential lifespan of 16 or more years, your Shih Tzu won't technically gain senior status until he is roughly 13 years old.

Why I Adore Shih Tzu

between 9 and 10.5 inches (23 and 27 cm). Proportion is key in this little dog—he should be well-balanced with no exaggerated features. With a level back and no apparent waist, a Shih Tzu should be slightly longer than he is tall. His legs are straight, well-boned, and muscular, and his feet should be well padded and pointed straight ahead.

The Shih Tzu has large, well-spaced eyes that set the tone for the dog's warm, sweet expression. The ears are also large and heavily coated. Generally the skin on the nose, lips, and eye rings should be black.

The Expert Knows

International Acclaim

If you adore your Shih Tzu, you're certainly not alone. In addition to being treasured by contemporary owners, this imperial breed has been revered for hundreds of years. Long ago the Dalai Lama, Tibet's spiritual leader, gave these dogs as gifts to Chinese emperors as part of a longstanding annual custom. Known as sacred dogs—literally little temple dogs—in Tibet, the breed maintained its venerated status in China, where one of the later rulers of the Manchu Dynasty, the Empress Dowager, was said to have personally supervised the breeding of her palace dogs.

Oh, That Coat!

Show dogs have a long, flowing double-coat that comes in a variety of striking colours and combinations. Although excessive trimming is considered a fault in the ring, some trimming is permitted to allow ease of movement. The hair on top of the head should be tied up, but groomers must be careful not to pull too tightly when performing this task. If your Shih Tzu is fussing with his hair accessory constantly, this is a sign that the elastic is too tight.

Whether your dog's hair is long and elegant or short and sassy, the tail is always carried in a curve over his back. Since the main purpose of the breed is companionship, temperament is actually one of the qualities for which this breed is judged. Nowhere are qualities such as an outgoing nature, friendly disposition, and sense of trust more apparent than in this dog's exuberant tail.

Hopelessly Devoted to You

Describing the "typical" Shih Tzu personality is like trying to describe a "typical" person—an impossible task. These multifaceted little canines can be as diverse as their owners—playful one moment, serious the next. You may find that your Shih Tzu has a relentless stubborn streak, or you might find that your Shih Tzu's amiable nature ends up teaching you a thing or two about patience and compassion. Some dogs are content warming their masters' feet, while others are so full of energy that sitting still for more than five minutes is far more than they can bear.

There are some traits, however, that are common to most members of this breed. In general these dogs are extremely outgoing. With a strong sense of self, the Shih Tzu thrives in an environment where he is the centre of attention, but whether this leads him to a life filled with friends and fun activities or he becomes the stereotypical spoiled lap dog depends primarily on his owner's approach. Because Shih Tzu tend to develop strong bonds with their owners, they can become extremely possessive of them if not properly socialised at a young age. They can also be especially prone to separation anxiety for this same reason.

Smarty Pants

Shih Tzu are highly intelligent—frequently smart enough to know the difference between what their owners want to teach them and which of these lessons are, in their opinion, worthy of their time. Food can be extremely useful motivators during training, but care must be given not to rely too heavily on edible rewards, or your diminutive Shih Tzu may become overweight rather quickly. Especially when it comes to these smaller canines, rewards should ideally be offered intermittently.

The Shih Tzu loves to be the centre of attention.

FAMILY-FRIENDLY TIP

SHIH TZU AND CHILDREN

Because of their diminutive size, having a Shih Tzu in a house with babies and toddlers can be a difficult situation. While children this age may have the best intentions, their lack of physical coordination poses a serious threat to a small breed. Even young children, who may understand the basic rules of how to treat a pet, can prompt a nip if they are too loud or if they accidentally move too quickly, startling the dog. Older kids, on the other hand, can be well suited to this energetic and playful breed. As one breeder explained it to me, "Shih Tzu love children who are respectful and gentle with them."

Whether you are purchasing a puppy or adopting a Shih Tzu, if you have a child, your number one priority must be selecting an even-tempered, well-socialised animal. Once you have found the right dog for your family, the next step is training. Enroll your new dog in a programme such as puppy class or basic obedience, and encourage your child to take an active role in this process. You must never entrust the care of any dog entirely to a child, but by empowering a young person with the knowledge of how to properly treat a pet – and affording him or her with some level of responsibility, you will lay the foundation for a lifelong love and respect for animals.

For decades psychologists have known that random rewards actually act as a more intense motivator than constant ones. Need more proof? Just visit a casino and watch all the people sitting patiently in front of the slot machines, waiting for their big payday. Other effective motivators include petting, praise, and play. For the right dog, his own tenacity can inspire him to work surprisingly hard to fulfill his owner's expectations. These little canines can attain impressive obedience titles or enjoy gratifying work as therapy dogs.

Personality Plus

Many owners assert that the Shih Tzu lacks the *attitude* of other small breeds. One breeder says, "They really do have a super personality—they are not a yappy, demanding breed at all. They are

Winning Colours

White Shih Tzu with coloured markings are especially common today. In the early twentieth century, the Empress Dowager's favourite colouring was honey gold with a white splash on the forehead—the most highly coveted markings of the breed during that time period. Interestingly, though, both the first and second-prize winners at the China Kennel Club show in 1930 were solid black.

very quiet at times and can entertain themselves if need be."

Haven't I Seen You Somewhere Before?

Well-known owners of the Shih Tzu breed include the late Frank Sinatra, singer Mariah Carey, and teen icon Nicole Richie.

Chapter 2

The Stuff of
Everyday Life

The first time I heard comedian George Carlin perform, he poked fun at the human tendency to treasure our *stuff*. I am reminded of this monologue whenever I watch my dog Molly trot over to her overflowing toy box and carefully make a selection. Stuff can indeed be as important to our dogs as it is to us—and they certainly need a lot of it, as evidenced by the growing pet supply industry. By using some simple guidelines, though, it is possible to get everything you need for your new Shih Tzu without breaking the bank or allowing it all to overrun your home.

14

Shih Tzu

W ith the seemingly unending number of new pet products appearing on the shelves of pet stores today, the key to making sure your Shih Tzu has what he needs is focusing on the few vital things in the beginning and saving the rest for later. You might find several additional items down the road that you just can't live without, but below are the ones that you will be glad you invested in first. Once your dog is housetrained and no longer teething, you can start to add to his *stuff*, and by then the chances will be better that he won't destroy them.

A Crate Is Great

I am always hesitant to assume that a dog owner will want to use a crate. I say this, because for many years I myself was very resistant to the idea, so I understand how critics of the crate feel. Yes, I too thought it was cruel. Yes, I vowed I would never put my dog in one. And yes, I now feel entirely differently about them.

It was actually my Molly who ultimately brought me around to the idea of trying a crate. When she was a puppy, Molly insisted on camping out below my desk where all my computer's power cords were gathered. I had to do something to keep her away from this hazardous area. I tried a baby gate, but she cried whenever I was working and she couldn't be with me. I tried holding her in my lap, but this was rather impractical. Finally, I broke down and bought a crate.

Two and a half years later it is still her favourite location for enjoying a new bone, stashing a new toy, or just napping whenever the mood strikes. Perhaps the greatest testament to the crate, though, was when my husband and I had to place our dogs in their crates for several hours while we installed a new floor in our home. With the exception of going outside periodically, Molly was in her kennel for most of the day. That evening as we stretched out on the sofa to rest our

Consistency Is Key

Bringing a new puppy into your home is not unlike having a new baby. And like babies, puppies thrive when kept on schedules. By making feeding, walking, and bedtime routine events in your pup's life, you give him the best advantage in getting used to his new household.

weary bones, Molly went back to her crate all on her own to take another snooze.

Size Matters

Crates can also come in extremely handy while housetraining, but remember that size is crucial. Making sure your dog's crate is big enough should be your first priority, but go just one size too large, and you will likely lose the housetraining advantage. Your Shih Tzu's crate should be spacious enough for him to stand up and turn around in, but not so roomy that he can decide to use one end as a makeshift bathroom.

Plastic or Wire?

When it comes to choosing between plastic and wire, several factors come into play. If your pup seeks out quieter, den-like spots in the house with low light and little noise, you probably want a plastic model, as these usually provide more privacy. Conversely, if your Shih Tzu likes to be in on all the household action, the wire is likely the better choice. If you plan to travel with your dog, be sure to buy an airline certified carrier, a

quality most wire crates lack, since they are collapsible.

Finally, don't forget to add something soft and comfy to the interior. A full array of crate liners is available at most pet supply stores. I strongly recommend having at least two, as they can then be rotated on laundry day.

Food and Water Bowls

All dogs need dishes, but which kind is best for your Shih Tzu? Good old-fashioned stainless steel is an eternal favourite and a smart option. In addition to being affordable, these metal bowls are durable, easy to clean, and pose no known health risks to dogs. Just be sure to select an appropriate size for this smaller breed, or

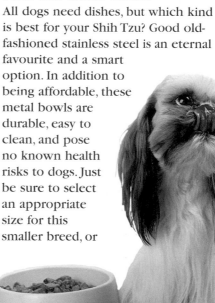

Plastic bowls are popular, but not always best.

15

The Stuff of Everyday Life

you just might find your Shih Tzu puppy climbing into

his dish to reach that last morsel of food.

While shopping you will see that ceramic and plastic are also popular materials for dog dishes. I recommend buying only table-quality ceramics intended for human use if you prefer this medium, since this is the only way to be certain that the product is not tainted with lead. Although plastic is durable and easily washed, it can lead to a condition called *plastic dish nasal dermatitis.* Caused by an antioxidant found in plastic, this contact dermatitis can cause your dog to lose the dark

pigmentation in his nose and lips. It can also cause swelling and irritation.

Collar

The most important thing to remember when selecting a collar for your Shih Tzu is that choke chains of any kind are unacceptable for this breed—period. If used incorrectly, a choke chain (also called a choke collar or training collar) can cause irreparable damage to your dog's delicate neck. Even when handled properly by an owner, it can easily injure a pulling dog who ignores the constriction, whether out of mere excitement or due to his own tenacity.

Collars made of nylon are usually the most versatile, since nylon is lightweight, easy to clean, and available in a wide selection of colours and patterns. Leather collars are also considerably durable, but most do not offer the added benefit of breakaway technology.

Although the average size collar for a Shih Tzu is 14 to 16 inches (35 to 40 cm), every dog is different. If your dog is especially small, a kitten collar may offer a better fit, particularly during puppyhood. You can use a measuring tape to determine the size of your dog's neck. Place the tape around his neck, but make sure you are able to fit two fingers comfortably between your Shih Tzu's neck and the tape.

Some Shih Tzu owners prefer to use a harness instead of a collar. Worn around the chest, a harness can help prevent a talented wriggler from escaping his owner. Like the collar, you can measure your Shih Tzu for

Little Helping Hands

Never leave a Shih Tzu entirely in the charge of a child. Even the best kid can forget to feed or walk a dog. Employing a set of checks and balances (literally) can be helpful. Post a list of all the things that need to be done on a daily basis, and have your child check off each task as it is completed. Younger children can certainly be involved in this process by assisting in feeding and cleaning up, but for the safety of all involved, please never leave a baby or toddler alone with any dog.

works wonderfully, as do extendable leads suited to your dog's size. The lead should afford your Shih Tzu with enough room to walk safely alongside you, but without his feeling restrictively tethered.

One advantage of using an extendable lead is that it mimics the freedom of running free, allowing your dog to explore his outdoor surroundings without being placed in harm's way. You must always remain vigilant when walking your dog, and shorten the line when walking in higher-traffic areas. Using this kind of lead is like having several different leads in one. Extendables are also quite

a harness, but instead of placing the measuring tape around the neck, it should be placed around your dog's chest, just behind his front legs.

Lead

When looking for a lead for your new Shih Tzu, examine the weight and length. Although you want a lead that is strong and secure, the lighter weight the better, since anything too heavy can be a burden for this tiny dog. Leather may work fine, but chain is inappropriate. Usually nylon

17

Your Shih Tzu's toys should be appropriately sized.

Shih Tzu

SENIOR DOG TIP

Helping an Older Shih Tzu Acclimatise

Any dog—even a puppy—needs an adjustment period after entering a new home, but an older dog may need a little extra time and patience. Some dogs may regress somewhat in their housetraining; others might have a hard time sleeping; still others may have no difficulties at all. The best thing you can do in any of these cases is spend time getting to know and bonding with your new Shih Tzu. This, more than anything else, will help ensure the best possible transition.

handy when training your dog to come when called, as you can let him venture out a bit while still retaining control over his compliance of the command.

Toys

To some people dog toys may seem like an indulgence, but like children every dog needs playthings. Toys make life more fun. They encourage exercise, stimulate your Shih Tzu both mentally and physically, and help entertain your dog when you cannot.

This doesn't mean that a dog should simply be handed a toy and left to amuse himself. Whenever you introduce a new toy, begin by showing your dog how to play with it. Roll or bounce a ball, and encourage him to run after it and return it to you. Buy scented tennis balls or flavoured bones. And never underestimate the power of a squeaker—dogs, particularly puppies, love things that make noise. After all, part of playtime means being able to be loud and spontaneous.

When selecting toys for your Shih Tzu, look for things that are appropriately sized. Your tiny dog will certainly need smaller toys than a larger breed, but beware of items that are *too* little, as they may pose a choking hazard. Likewise, if your dog is an avid chewer, make sure you confiscate any pieces that break off or become dangerously loose.

Bed

Although many owners readily share their beds with their dogs, the decision to allow your Shih Tzu to sleep with you is not merely an issue of whether the dog should be allowed on the furniture. With a Shih Tzu's smaller stature, a tall bed can be a precarious place. A single jump or fall could cause a broken leg or other serious injury. If your dog must sleep in your bed, consider buying a toddler-sized stepstool and training your dog to use it whenever getting on or off the bed.

A better place for your dog to sleep is in a bed of his own. Dog beds are

A fabulous bed or couch of his own can have your Shih Tzu sitting pretty.

available in a huge variety of fabrics and styles, but functionality should always take precedence. If the bed isn't comfortable, your dog won't use it. An older Shih Tzu may appreciate a bed made from orthopedic foam or the new memory foam so popular in those trendy mattresses. If your dog uses a crate, this is also a very safe spot for your Shih Tzu overnight. Likewise, it can serve as an efficient starter bed for a puppy that may likely ruin a conventional dog bed.

Gates

It's a great idea for all owners to invest in a quality safety gate. This is one of the most useful pieces of equipment you may ever buy. Until your Shih Tzu learns to climb stairs, it can be a life-saving device. It can also help protect your carpeting and furniture until your Shih Tzu is housetrained. If you prefer not to crate, I strongly recommend using a gate.

Several styles are sold in most pet supply stores. You can also find gates in the baby section of most department stores. If you will be using the gate in the same location all the time, a mountable swing-style model may be the most convenient choice. If you want to use the gate in several different areas of your home, look for a spring-

Doggie Daycare

Few owners are able to stay home with their dogs 24 hours a day. Some dogs deal with time spent alone quite well. Many others, however, will pine if they are left for long periods.

No dog should be left on its own for longer than four hours at a stretch. Obviously, this applies to adult dogs only. Puppies cannot be left alone, even when crated, for longer than two hours.

If you have a job that means you have to leave your dog for longer than four hours, you will need to find a dog sitter who will come to your home. This may be a friendly neighbour, but in most cases you will need to employ a professional dog sitter. The dog sitter will give your dog exercise, play with him, and feed him if necessary.

In order to find a reliable, trustworthy pet sitter in your area, log on to www.dogservices.co.uk or www.ukpetsitter.com

mounted model. Some styles even offer the option of using them either way. Gates are available in plastic, wood, and metal. Although metal is the most durable, any of these should work well for your Shih Tzu. Avoid accordion-style models, though, as these pose a strangulation hazard.

Exercise Pens (X-pen)

I always used to think of exercise pens as being for breeders only. While it's true that most breeders do use x-pens for keeping puppies safe during outside play, they are also fantastic devices for pet owners. Usually consisting of eight foldable sides, x-pens are easy to assemble, can be used inside or outside, and provide all the same safety benefits of a baby gate with the added advantage of being freestanding.

Grooming Supplies

Whether you plan to have a professional groom your dog or you will be grooming your Shih Tzu personally, you will need a few tools for daily maintenance. By far the two most important grooming aids you will ever purchase are a good brush and comb. Look for a slicker brush with a curved back and a metal comb. You needn't buy the most expensive items available, but know that extremely cheap tools are often worth what you pay for them.

Another item you will need frequently is a pair of nail clippers. Overgrown nails not only hurt your dog, but they can also cause your dog

Last, but Not Least

Once you have all the things you need for your new Shih Tzu, remember that what your dog needs most is someone to make good decisions on his behalf. This means not only buying things like collars with breakaway technology and the proper grooming tools, but also using them. As your dog's owner, your job is to keep him safe, fit, and healthy. Always keep your Shih Tzu on his lead when in an unfenced area, don't overlook vital grooming tasks (such as brushing his teeth), and perhaps most importantly, make time for daily periods of exercise and play. His physical and mental health depend on it.

toothbrush are useful, though not necessary. I brush my own dogs' teeth with a gauze-wrapped index finger, and they tolerate this better than a conventional brush. Although so much of grooming is about keeping your dog looking good, grooming also helps keep your dog healthy. There is nothing pretty about infected ears or tooth decay. When it comes to keeping your dog looking good, remember that cleanliness is next to dogliness.

Identification

It seems impossible that you shold ever lose your precious Shih Tzu, but it does happen. If your dog is ever lost, an identification tag could mean the difference between getting him back or not. A tag or disc bearing your name and contact information

to injure himself and others. By the time you can hear your dog's nails hitting the floor, they havc already grown past the point of needing trimming. Clippers come in three basic designs—pliers-style, guillotine-style, and scissors-style. Which type is best is purely a matter of personal preference.

Finally, your Shih Tzu will also need a quality shampoo, ear cleanser, and toothpaste. Conditioners and a

Proper grooming supplies are necessary for daily maintenance of your Shih Tzu's coat.

can enable anyone who may find your Shih Tzu to return him to you at once. These tags have become extremely inexpensive and accessible. Most pet stores have a service providing an engraved tag with your dog's name and your own, as well as your address and phone number.

Microchipping

But what if your dog is stolen instead of lost? How can you prevent someone from removing your dog's tags? Unfortunately, you cannot, which is why microchipping has become such a popular option among pet owners. Unlike a tattoo, which can also be grain of rice, is placed under your dog's skin in a process as quick and painless as a vaccination. Once inserted, it is detectable only with the use of a handheld electronic device used by rescue centres and vets who read your dog's unique identification number.

Be sure to register your dog's number with the related company, though, or else this number will have no value. You must also inform the company any time your address or phone number changes. Likewise, if you change vets, inform your new vet that your dog has been micropchipped and provide the number for the new hospital's records.

It's the Law

It is a legal requirement that every dog should carry some form of identification, giving owner contact details.

Keep your dog safe—if your Shih Tzu is outside off lead, he needs to be in a fenced-in area.

altered, a microchip is the best way of ensuring that your dog will be returned to you, his rightful owner, if someone else ever tries to claim him. The microchip, which is approximately the size of a

Chapter 3

Good Eating

What exactly is a balanced canine diet? Just like you, your Shih Tzu needs a healthy combination of protein, carbohydrates, and fatty acids along with a number of different vitamins and minerals. These nutrients fuel your dog's basic body systems and help keep him looking and feeling in tip-top shape.

Your Shih Tzu needs a healthy combination of protein, carbohydrates, and fatty acids.

Water

The first step in providing your Shih Tzu with proper nutrition is undoubtedly the easiest. Make sure your dog is given unlimited access to fresh, clean water. This simple task will help maintain a normal body temperature, transport vital nutrients throughout the body, and help eliminate undesired substances in the form of urine.

Your dog needs water regardless of where he is, so always take some along wherever you go. A simple metal bowl and a hose is all you need to keep your Shih Tzu from getting dehydrated while playing in the garden. If you take your dog hiking or for long walks, you can purchase a collapsible bowl that can be filled during a rest period and tucked away when not in use.

Protein

Found in such foods as meat, fish, eggs, milk, and legumes, protein is essential for the growth and repair of body tissue. It also helps maintain the framework that holds the calcium in your dog's bones and teeth. Protein even helps produce antibodies, your dog's best defense against bacteria, viruses, and toxic substances.

Carbohydrates

Although we have been virtually programmed in recent years to think of carbohydrates as a bad thing, they are a very common part of many commercial pet foods. An excellent source of calories, carbs serve as an efficient source of energy. Although they are not technically required in a canine diet, carbohydrates aid in digestion, therefore serving an important role in your Shih Tzu's dietary plan.

Fats

Fats have also got a bad press from us humans, but they are also surprisingly important to your Shih Tzu. These athletic little dogs convert fat into energy at a very impressive rate. Rather than storing it like people do, Shih Tzus convert fat into energy within just hours. If your dog doesn't exercise regularly, he will be more likely to gain weight, but even a couch potato pooch will require a higher percentage of fat in his diet than his human counterparts.

Vitamins and Minerals

Vitamins and minerals are given a whole lot of lip service, but rarely do we hear which ones our dogs should be getting. The primary canine vitamins are A, D, E, B complex, and K. If you have any trouble remembering these, just think of this phrase: *A Dog Enjoys Being Kind.* If feeding a prepackaged food, you want to look for these vitamins on the food label, or you can feed fresh foods such as liver, fish, green leafy vegetables, and egg yolks, which contain an ample amount of these vitamins.

Calcium

Calcium is one of the most important minerals for dogs of all ages. In addition to helping maintain strong bones and teeth, calcium is also responsible for certain nerve functions. If your Shih Tzu's calcium intake is too low, this can also increase his risk of joint problems. Most dairy products offer a significant amount of calcium, but some dogs have a hard time digesting these foods. Fortunately, calcium can also be found in vegetables such as broccoli, sweet potatoes, and leafy greens—all practical alternatives for dairy-intolerant canines.

What to Avoid

Perhaps the more important information is which vitamins you should *not* give your Shih Tzu. These include supplemental vitamin C—ascorbic acid, sodium ascorbate, calcium ascorbate or ascorbal palmitate; as these can cause damage to your dog's liver and kidneys. Although

Supplements

If your Shih Tzu is in good health and eating a well balanced diet, vitamins and mineral supplements should not be required. When given indiscriminately, in fact, many can be dangerous. If you think your dog may benefit from a particular supplement, talk to your vet *before* offering it. The best way to offer any vitamin or mineral is in the form of a food containing it, so make the selection of your dog's basic diet your first priority.

Interestingly, foods containing vitamin E have been shown to help fight cancer in human patients, but this property appears absent when given in supplement form. And remember that sometimes nutrients are provided in unexpected ways. Vitamin D, for example, is found in sunshine.

vitamin A is necessary for preventing eye and skin problems, it can be toxic when given in excess. Selenium, while beneficial to the canine heart, can also be toxic when given in doses disproportionate to your dog's weight.

Abstain from offering vitamins or minerals in supplement form unless your vet recommends them. This may be the case if your Shih Tzu has entered his geriatric years or if he is suffering from an illness. If your dog is young and healthy, however, a well balanced diet should provide all the nutrients his body needs—without the danger of consuming too much of any one in particular.

Owners must exercise caution even when providing vitamins by way of fresh foods. While the excess amount of a water-soluble vitamin usually passes through your dog's system, fat-soluble vitamins can be stored and build up within your Shih Tzu's body, unnoticed until they have already caused a problem. Feeding in moderation is always best. Too much of anything can be bad, even a healthy food.

Prepackaged Foods

Once you know which nutrients your Shih Tzu needs, you must decide what type of diet you prefer. Unfortunately, there is no single plan that can be recommended for every dog—not even those of the same breed. Age, lifestyle, and even personality can play a role. The choices can

seem endless. After you settle on a brand, you will then have to select from high-energy formulas, dental-friendly varieties, and low-calorie regimens for more rotund pups. There are even vegetarian options available.

Dry Food

Dry food is the most popular choice for owners purchasing a commercial food. This makes sense, as the advantages are numerous. Dry food can be stored in bulk without waste, and it is easy to feed since it requires virtually no preparation. Owners can feed their dogs a certain amount at a specific time, or they can leave a full bowl available throughout the day.

Canned Food

Take a walk through your local pet supply store, and you will see that canned food is also a very popular choice among dog owners. This medium also has its advantages. Like dry dog food, canned or wet food can easily be purchased in advance without worry of spoilage.

Make sure your dog is given unlimited access to fresh, clean water.

However, allowing wet food to sit in your dog's bowl for long periods of time is not a safe option for your pet. Leftovers should always be refrigerated until your dog's next meal.

You will also need to make sure that you brush your dog's teeth frequently if he is on a canned regimen. Feeding crunchy treats will definitely help, but wet food has a way of jumping on the fast track to morphing into calculus, the clinical term for tartar. Often this is not even visible until it has already solidified. Canned food can also mean looser stools. This doesn't affect your dog's health, but it can be rather unpleasant for the person in charge of garden cleanup.

Semi-moist Food

While dry and wet foods always each seem to have their die-hard supporters who prefer one kind to the other, semi-moist regimens tend to have more critics than enthusiasts. Although your dog may be more than willing to finish every morsel of this attractively packaged meal (many are sculpted into burger shapes), most semi-moist foods contain excessive amounts of sugar. Not only is this bad for your Shih Tzu's teeth, but it is also especially

dangerous for dogs with diabetes or weight problems (a risk factor for the disease).

If your dog likes the flavour of a semi-moist food, a healthy alternative to the mainstream options is something called a dog food roll. Packaged similar to salamis, these foods offer a compromise—pleasant taste *and* good nutrition. As with any type of food, though, you must check the label to make sure the brand is nutritionally sound.

Making Sense of Food Labels

Although manufacturers are required by law to list ingredients in descending order according to weight, this method can be misleading. You may read the first ingredient—chicken, for example—and assume that you have chosen a food that consists mostly of just that: chicken. However, if byproducts are subdivided into several different categories, they can still outweigh the healthier ingredients. Ideally, you want no byproducts in

FAMILY-FRIENDLY TIP

"Can I Help—Please?"

Kids always want to help with new puppies, but you may wonder which tasks are age-appropriate. Even a toddler can help feed your new Shih Tzu, and the benefits are two-fold. While showing your child how to kindly interact with an animal, you will also be helping your Shih Tzu pup form a positive connotation to children. After measuring out a meal's worth of dry food, instruct your son or daughter to offer the food one piece at a time by hand. Praise the puppy for taking these morsels gently. While every meal does not have to be presented this way, a hand-feeding technique will also help prevent the problem of food aggression.

your dog's food, but you certainly don't want them to prevail over what appears to be the main ingredient.

In the UK, pet food is controlled by the Food Standards Agency (FSA), which has to adhere to EC guidelines. Manufacturers also belong to the Pet Food Manufacturers' Association (PFMA), which, in turn, follows guidelines laid down by the European Pet Food Industry Federation (FEDIAF).

A phone number listed on the package is an excellent means of getting answers to any questions you may have about a particular food. And don't forget to check another critical number—the bag's expiration date.

The most important thing to remember is if your dog is thriving on his current food, you needn't rush into making any changes at all. If, after doing some research, you do find a better option by all means switch, but be sure to make the change gradually to avoid stomach upset.

Alternative Feeding Choices

Homecooked Diet

When I was growing up, my mother cooked for our Poodle. No, I don't mean that she gave him the family's leftovers. He did often eat what we were eating, but his portion wasn't what was left over after dinner; he ate with us. And if we happened to be having a meal that was inappropriate for him—anything with onions, for instance—she would either make him a separate batch of the same recipe (without the onions) or another dish altogether. In the 1980s, this seemed odd to many of our friends, but my mother insisted that it was the best way to make sure he was getting all the nutrients he needed. This is the very premise of what is now referred to as a homecooked canine diet.

Although it may seem like it would be more expensive than buying a bag of dry food every few weeks, homecooking can be surprisingly economical—especially if owners peruse their weekly grocery store flyers for the best deals. One must make certain, however, that a balanced diet is provided. Practically any dog will enjoy the variety provided from a homecooked diet, but if vital nutrients are absent from the menu, your dog's optimum health will ultimately be sacrificed.

Dogs eating homecooked meals exclusively will also need their teeth brushed more often than those that eat dry food. Although some foods may be on the firmer side (vegetables or pasta cooked al dente, for instance), most will be comparable to the consistency of canned food. You may also need to add or eliminate certain ingredients from your dog's individual diet to help firm up or soften his stools, but a happy medium is achievable.

Raw Diet

The concept of feeding a dog a diet comprised strictly of raw foods may at first seem rather primitive. The basis for this style of feeding that has become extremely popular in recent years, however, makes a lot of sense. Simply put, raw foods retain more of their innate health-enhancing benefits that cooking eradicates. Sometimes referred to by its acronym, the BARF diet (short for *bones and raw food*) inspires immediate images of blood-red meat and bones, and this certainly is part of the regimen. When used properly, however, one sees that meat is just one element in a very carefully designed and balanced diet. Other raw foods included in this plan are eggs, poultry, fish, fruit, and vegetables.

Many breeders and vets recommend the BARF diet. Just as the advantages of this diet are numerous, though,

Children can help with feeding the dog, but it's up to a responsible adult to make sure it happens every day.

Free feeding can be problematic in multiple dog households.

so are the liabilities—as evidenced by the comparable number of canine health professionals who strongly discourage the practice of feeding raw food. Small breeds in particular are at considerable risk of suffering from broken teeth or intestinal injuries from bone fragments, but dogs of all sizes can experience these unfortunate injuries. A dog eating raw meat may also come in contact with such dangerous bacteria as salmonella and E. coli.

If you think feeding raw food is worth the risk, be sure to do thorough research before changing your dog to an exclusively raw plan. As with homecooking, balance is key with BARF. If you don't do your homework, you can miss all the benefits that this regimen should provide—or worse, put your dog's health at risk due to a particular nutritional component that has been overlooked.

Free Feeding or Scheduled Feeding?

Is it better to feed your Shih Tzu on a schedule, or "free feed," in which he is provided with a constant supply of food to consume whenever he wishes? In my opinion scheduled feeding is the best way to ensure that your dog is getting as much food as he needs without allowing him to gorge himself, something I am certain my own dogs would do if given the opportunity. Watching your dog's weight may seem like a good indicator that he is eating the right amount, but if a health crisis strikes, you won't know for certain how much his appetite has been affected. Erratic eating habits can also make housetraining exceptionally more challenging.

Of course, some dogs do fine on a free feeding routine. Free feeding is often problematic, however, if your dog is prone to weight gain or in multiple pet households, where an older or bigger animal can bully another out of his fair share. While free feeding may work for singletons without a gluttonous streak, it can also be counterproductive for dogs that have lost their zest for food.

Owners who opt for free feeding mustn't overlook the importance of washing their dogs' dishes regularly. Although it may be tempting to just

A *Lifetime* of *Good Nutrition*

Puppies Up to Four Months

Younger puppies need more protein than older dogs. They also need to eat more frequently. Feed your new Shih Tzu puppy three times a day, dividing the total amount of food given among these meals. Offer water with each meal, but while you are house-training, be sure to remove it about an hour or two before bedtime.

Puppies Between Four Months and One Year

Once your Shih Tzu puppy reaches four months of age, you can eliminate his mid-day meal. Somewhere between the ages of 9 and 12 months, your pup should be swapped over to an adult food. Although larger breeds aren't ready for this transition until they are between one and two years old, smaller breeds reach their adult size well before this time, thus requiring less protein. As soon as housetraining is complete, you can also begin offering water at all times.

Adult Shih Tzu (1 to 12 years)

Most adult Shih Tzu should eat two meals per day. Look for diets specially formulated for smaller breeds. Not only will these regimens contain the specific combination of nutrients your Shih Tzu needs, but the food will also be sized more appropriately for your smaller dog's mouth than standard diets. You can offer variety in the form of healthy snacks like raw vegetables. Just be sure to watch your dog's weight, as metabolism slows with age. Superfluous pounds will only be harder to lose as your Shih Tzu approaches his senior years.

Senior Shih Tzu (approx 13 years and up)

The senior Shih Tzu's diet is perhaps the most individualised of all age groups. If your dog has any health concerns, your veterinarian may recommend feeding a specialty diet. If your dog is in good health, he may need a change of some other sort to renew his interest in eating. Wet food or home-cooking can often help with this. Since a Shih Tzu's nutritional needs (and metabolism) change once again at this time, changing to a food made specifically for seniors is a good idea. You may also want to discontinue feeding harder foods if your dog's teeth are in poor shape or if he is missing teeth.

Exercise, play, and a balanced diet can help keep your Shih Tzu in shape.

top up the food every morning, don't. Bacteria and other germs grow rapidly on bowls that are left to stagnate. To retain the convenience factor, simply purchase two sets of dishes for your Shih Tzu and rotate them daily whenever you feed your dog, leaving the chore of cleaning to your dishwasher.

Obesity

One of the most fundamental responsibilities of dog ownership is to provide adequate nutrition. Stories of neglected pets denied basic sustenance are horrifying to compassionate pet owners. What many people don't realise, though, is that overfeeding a pet can be almost as

dangerous to health as this more overt form of abuse. Allowing a dog to become obese is one of the cruelest things an owner can do. The excessive portions may be doled out with love, but remember that sometimes kindness can kill.

As it is in humans, obesity is a contributing factor to countless canine diseases and other chronic conditions, including problems with the heart, lungs, liver, kidneys, bones and joints. Being overweight can even lower your dog's immune system. Unlike larger breeds, your Shih Tzu will reach the point of obesity with the addition of just a few extra pounds.

The two biggest causes of obesity are overeating and lack of exercise.

In order to keep your dog at his ideal weight, you must assume the roles of both his personal nutritionist and trainer. Weighing your dog or checking his ribs regularly can be especially helpful. Place a hand on each side of your dog's body to see if you can feel his ribs—they should be discernable, though not prominent. If your dog is already carrying extra weight, talk to your vet before beginning a more rigorous exercise routine, but whatever you do, don't put it off! It is never too late to get your dog back into shape.

Creating Good Table Manners

Your Shih Tzu won't develop good table manners unless you're willing to teach him. When owners tolerate behaviours such as begging or growling, they reinforce these actions. Rewarding a dog with the food he is seeking is an even stronger reinforcement. Punishment, however, is not the answer. If your dog begs for your food, simply remove him from the room. Certainly, you should give him an opportunity to behave better next time, but be consistent in your handling of the situation, and any problem will likely become a thing of the past.

This does not mean you cannot share. Offering healthy food from your meals won't have a negative impact on your Shih Tzu's table manners, providing that you remember a few basic rules. First, never offer tastes directly from the table. Instead, place your dog's portion into his bowl from the counter area. Second, remember the worst time to give in to begging is after you have initially refused and your dog has continued beseeching you. This teaches him that the payoff is worth a stubborn effort.

Finally, be watchful of snappy reactions. If your dog begins acting aggressively when given food of any kind, stop using a bowl and begin hand-feeding at once. If the problem persists, consult your vet or an animal behaviourist.

The Expert Knows

Can Treats Be Part of a Healthy Diet?

Healthy treats can be a great addition to any canine diet, but since most dogs don't possess a great amount of self-discipline, owners must exercise control over which and how many treats their dogs consume. If you are concerned that your Shih Tzu is consuming too many treats, keep track by setting aside what you think should be a full day's portion and stick to this measured amount.

Shih Tzu

Feeding the Older Dog

As your Shih Tzu enters his senior years, you may notice that he isn't as enthusiastic about mealtime as he once was. Ageing affects many aspects of your dog's life, including his sense of taste. As a dog ages, his taste buds become less sensitive. Additionally, your older dog is likely losing muscle strength and bone mass, so good nutrition is especially vital to his good health. If the change seems sudden (or is accompanied by other symptoms), consult your vet. If a waning appetite is gradual, however, trying some of these tricks may bring your dog back to his bowl:

- Warm up your dog's wet food, or add some water to dry food, heating it before serving. By doing so, you will release the meal's aroma. This can also make food easier to chew, which may be a concern for your older dog.

- Instead of feeding your elderly dog just once or twice daily, consider dividing his food into several smaller meals. Keep the choices healthy, but avoid hard foods such as raw vegetables, which may be more difficult to chew.

- Because he is now less efficient at metabolising protein, your senior dog needs more of this nutrient. As long as your dog is not suffering from kidney disease (in which case you would want to limit protein), you might be able to lure your older dog back into eating by adding foods such as meat and fish to the menu. Cottage cheese and hard-boiled eggs are also enticing protein-rich additions that can be added to the daily grind.

SENIOR DOG TIP

Eat Together!

According to a recent study on neurobiology and ageing by the University of Toronto, it is the combination of a healthy diet and a stimulating environment that helps an older dog maintain his mental acuity. Like people, dogs are social creatures, so don't feed your dog in the kitchen while the family gathers around the dining room table. Eat together, and make sure you take a walk or indulge in a play session when the meal is done. Diet is just one part of a healthy lifestyle that helps makes longevity possible!

Good Eating

Chapter 4

Looking Good

When a dog looks good, he knows it. It shows in the way he carries himself. A well-groomed dog is confident, comfortable, and ready to strut his stuff. By keeping your Shih Tzu properly groomed, you show him that you love him and want to give him the very best care. In addition to the many compliments you will receive on your Shih Tzu's appearance, keeping up with these basic tasks also offers you the peace of mind of knowing that your dog is in the best possible health.

Brushing

Brushing your Shih Tzu may seem like a simple task, yet when overlooked, it can become one of the most difficult grooming chores you could ever imagine. When not properly cared for, the long silky outer coat and the soft, dense undercoat of this breed are especially prone to matting. Knots making it all the way down to the skin can be nearly impossible to loosen, leaving owners with the unpleasant option of shaving their dogs to remove these severe tangles. The best way to avoid this problem is to brush your dog as often as possible.

The Right Tools

One of the biggest mistakes many owners make is simply running the brush over the top of their dogs' coats. In order to rid your dog of the dead skin and hair, dirt, and snarls buried deep within his fur, you must reach this area with the right type of brush. A slicker brush with a curved back is ideal for your Shih Tzu's coat, but you will achieve the best results by following up brushing with combing your dog. The comb is an excellent indicator that you have done a thorough job brushing your Shih Tzu. If you have missed any tangles beneath the

Follow up brushing your Shih Tzu with combing.

Shih Tzu

top layer of fur, a comb will surely let you know that you need to repeat this task.

Line Brushing

Many groomers familiar with this breed recommend using a method known as *line brushing*. Starting at your Shih Tzu's foot, brush a small layer of hair upwards exposing a line of skin that designates a small section of fur. Brush this area thoroughly, first up and then back down. Moving upwards, work on one section of fur at a time in this way until you have brushed the entire leg. Continue this on the remaining legs, back, chest, and belly.

The time required for this task will depend on the length of your dog's hair. You can expect to spend about an hour brushing a Shih Tzu in full coat, considerably less for a dog kept in a pet clip. Likewise, you will need to brush a dog with longer hair more often, ideally at least once every day. Special attention should always be paid to the areas behind your dog's ears and where the legs join the chest and belly, as these spots are particularly prone to matting. A coat spray designed to combat tangles—or even a fine mist of water—may help make the job easier, but be careful not to use too much.

Bathing

Although opinions differ as to how often a dog should be bathed, you can safely shampoo your Shih Tzu as frequently as necessary. If your dog spends a lot of time outdoors, this may

Your Shih Tzu's Bag of Grooming Tricks

Items a well-groomed Shih Tzu should never be without:

- Slicker brush
- Metal comb
- Canine shampoo and conditioner
- Ear cleaning solution
- Toothpaste and toothbrush (or gauze)
- Nail clippers
- Styptic powder (or other clot-speeding substance)

mean giving baths as often as once every week or two. If you keep up with the task of brushing—one of the best ways of removing dirt and debris from your dog's coat—you may find that a bath is only necessary every four to six weeks. However often you plan to bathe your Shih Tzu, start the process early. A dog that has had regular baths since he was a puppy is much more likely to accommodate his owner during the process.

The most important rule of bathing is that you should never move on to this task until you have brushed your Shih Tzu completely. Bathing a matted dog will only make the problem worse. Even if your dog only has a few minor tangles, these too will be nearly impossible to remove once your dog has been bathed, so take the extra time to make sure you have done a

Looking Good

Never bathe your Shih Tzu without brushing him first.

benefit of a sink sprayer within easy reach, and doesn't require any bending on behalf of the person in charge. It is imperative, though, that you never leave your dog unattended either in the sink or on your countertop, as a fall from this height could be catastrophic.

Other options include using your bathtub or purchasing a separate bathing tub. (I recently bathed my own dogs at my breeder's house, and I must say that my back much preferred the elevated tub in her grooming room to the conventional bathroom tub I use to bathe my dogs at home.)

Supplies

Before bathing your Shih Tzu, gather all the necessary supplies—an absorbent towel, a soft washcloth, shampoo, cotton-wool balls, mineral oil, and a cup for rinsing if you do not have a sprayer attachment. Once your dog is in the water, you won't be able to run back for a forgotten item, so go over your list twice before getting started. Once you are certain you have everything you'll need, check to make sure the room temperature is sufficient, and fill the basin with warm water. You can check

thorough job before running that bath water.

Where Should I Bathe My Shih Tzu?

Many Shih Tzu owners bathe their dogs right in their kitchen sink. This space is usually large enough, has the added this temperature the same way you would a baby's bath water—with your elbow.

How to Bathe Your Shih Tzu

Before placing your dog in the water, gently position one cotton-wool ball in each of your dog's ears to prevent water from entering this area. Now your dog is ready for the water. After wetting his coat, pour a small amount of shampoo into your hand and work it into your Shih Tzu's fur, forming a lather. Your dog's shampoo won't yield the same amount of suds as your own shampoo. This makes it easier for you to rinse it thoroughly from his coat. Always use a quality canine shampoo on your Shih Tzu—never a product made for humans.

Once you have finished washing, drain the sink or tub and start the rinsing process. The best way to ensure proper rinsing is repeating the process several times, even if you feel certain you have already done a thorough job. Even a small amount of suds left in your dog's coat can cause itchy, dry skin. If you will be using a conditioner, this is time to apply it—rinsing your dog carefully once again.

Next, wet your washcloth and gently wash your dog's face with plain water. When you are done, you can

After the bath, towel dry your Shih Tzu and follow up with brushing.

then remove the cotton-wool balls from your Shih Tzu's ears and gently wipe the insides with mineral water.

Drying

Now your Shih Tzu is ready to be dried, first with a towel and then with a hairdryer on a low-heat setting. (If

Isn't it Time for My Bath?

Grooming is a trust-building activity. Certainly, it takes some time for a young Shih Tzu to get used to the many tasks involved, but few things are as gratifying as watching a dog make the transition from a nervous puppy who baulks at the idea of having a single toenail trimmed to a composed adult that stands readily for brushing and bathing. I have found that in a multi-dog household, grooming is very special one-on-one time. My dog, Molly, who fussed for the duration of her first bath at home, now holds a grudge if the tub I draw is *not* for her.

your dog dislikes the dryer, try placing a fresh pair of cotton-wool balls back in his ears to muffle the sound.) Gently brush your dog throughout this time, keeping your arm safely in the airflow of the dryer to be certain it isn't too hot or too close to your dog's vulnerable skin. Allowing your dog to air-dry may seem like an easier option, but this can be problematic, since

the likelihood of tangles forming is significantly higher this way.

Nail Care

Your Shih Tzu's nails need regular attention. If you do not feel comfortable trimming them yourself, make sure you bring your dog to a professional. Both groomers and vets usually offer this service at a nominal fee. Regardless of who assumes the task, make sure it gets done before your dog's nails grow too long. By the time you can hear your dog's toenails when he walks across the floor, they are usually overdue for a trimming.

Although it can be a bit intimidating at first, owners can learn to cut their dogs nails themselves. The most important thing to remember is that trimming just a little more frequently is highly preferable to cutting off a large amount at any one time. By staying on top of this task, you will actually be lessening the risk of injuring your dog, for the more frequently the nail is cut, the more the quick (also called the nailbed) recedes. This is the pink area that bleeds if accidentally snipped.

How to Trim Your Shih Tzu's Nails

Place your dog in standing position, holding his foot firmly and pressing gently on the pad to extend the nail. It is easier to see the quick on nails that are light in colour, but unfortunately individual dogs frequently have a combination of light and dark-

coloured nails—
sometimes even
on the same
foot. Using your
clippers, snip off
just the hook-like
end of the nail on
a 45-degree angle. Especially if you
cannot discern the quick, err on the
side of caution.

Moisture and bacteria can accumulate quickly in your Shih Tzu's heavily coated ears if they aren't cleaned often.

Continue this method until all the
nails on the foot have been trimmed.
For a puppy, it may take several days
to finish all four feet, but the more
often you trim, the more he will get
used to having this important job done.
Touching your dog's feet at other times
will also help get him used to having
his feet handled—a huge hurdle in
the tolerance factor, so gently massage
his paws as often as possible while
he's young. Giving in to wiggling or
whining by postponing the task

will only teach your dog that these
tactics work, so be persistent.

The more often you trim, the more your Shih Tzu will get used to having this important job done.

What If You Cut the Quick?

If you do the trimming yourself,
chances are that you will accidentally
cut the quick at least once. When
this happens, remain calm and apply
direct pressure to the area for 10 to 15
minutes with a sterile towel
soaked in cold water. If the bleeding
persists, you may use a styptic powder,
pad, or pencil to speed clotting.
Other items that may be substituted
include a soft bar of soap,
cornstarch, or a wet tea bag. Finally,
if you seem to be cutting the quick
more often than not, consider
leaving the job to a professional.
Your dog will
easily forgive
an occasional
mishap, but
repeated injuries
may well result in

Looking Good

Do I Need a Grooming Table?

The answer to this question depends on several factors. Certainly, if you plan to show your Shih Tzu in conformation, a grooming table will be a virtual necessity. Likewise, if you plan to keep your pet Shih Tzu in a full coat, a table will come in extremely handy. Offering a non-skid surface, rounded corners, and a grooming arm for attaching a safety strap, a grooming table is highly preferable to placing your dog on a counter or other dangerously high surface in your home. There are even portable table-top versions, which can turn these surfaces into safer places for owners who lack the space for a more conventional grooming area. Most full-size tables fold for convenient storage and are lightweight for easy portability. Another advantage to having this elevated spot for grooming is that it helps many dogs behave. You can certainly brush your Shih Tzu in the middle of your living room floor, but can your dog differentiate grooming time from playtime in this multi-use environment?

Owners of dogs with shorter haircuts may not need to invest in this item unless their dogs find it difficult to tolerate the grooming process elsewhere. Unlike a smooth-coated breed, even a Shih Tzu with a short coat will need frequent brushing and regular nail trims, so don't overlook this useful tool that just might cut your grooming time in half.

a fear of nail trimming or a dangerous infection.

Nail Grinders

Many people prefer using a rotary grinding tool to more conventional nail clippers. These handheld devices are available at most pet supply stores and are either electric or battery-powered. The advantages to using one of these tools are numerous. For one thing, they tend to be quicker to use than clippers, a perk both you and your Shih Tzu will enjoy. Also, since they grind instead of cut, there is less chance of injuring your dog. If by chance too much nail *is* taken off, the wound is instantly cauterised. No matter which tool you prefer, it is a good idea to have a vet or professional groomer show you the right way to use this equipment before trying it yourself.

Ear Care

Bath day is certainly one of the most convenient times to clean your dog's ears, but this mustn't be the only time you perform this important task. Air flows easily into the upright ears of certain breeds like the German Shepherd and the Corgi but moisture and bacteria can accumulate quickly in your Shih Tzu's heavily coated ears if they aren't cleaned often. Ideally ear cleaning should be done about twice a week, but depending on your dog's tendency towards otitis externa (ear infection), it may even need to be done more often.

How to Clean Your Shih Tzu's Ears

Begin by squirting a small amount of ear cleanser into your Shih Tzu's ear. If you dog shakes his head, don't worry—this can only help spread the solution and loosen any debris within the ear. Next, massage the ear gently from the exterior and using cotton-wool balls wipe the ear from the inside out until the cotton-wool comes out clean. (This part of the task will need to be repeated several times. Leaving a small amount of wax in the ear actually helps keep the canal properly coated, so don't panic if you never get a piece of pristine cotton-wool.)

Unlike a human's anatomy, your dog's ear canal includes a 90-degree turn that marks the transition from his external ear canal to the more delicate inner ear. As long as you don't reach beyond this discernible barrier, you shouldn't cause any harm while cleaning your dog's ears. Also, never use a cotton bud in your dog's ears. In addition to being less efficient than a cotton-wool ball, a bud can easily injure your dog's ear canal if he jerks his head during the cleaning process.

If your Shih Tzu's ears show irritation from normal cleaning, isopropyl alcohol or hydrogen peroxide may be the culprit. Even a small amount of these ingredients can burn, especially if an infection is present. Try using a product free of these compounds, or use a homemade solution of water and vinegar instead (mixed to a 1:1 ratio).

SENIOR DOG TIP

Looking Good for Years to Come

You may find that grooming your older Shih Tzu takes a bit more time than it once did. Not only will your dog tire more easily as he ages, but you may also need to slow down your approach so as not to aggravate any lumps or bumps common to the geriatric years. Perhaps what you were able to accomplish in 10 minutes when your dog was an active adult will now take 20 minutes. Remain patient, and continue to praise your dog for tolerating grooming—even if this means spreading out a full nail clipping over several hours or days. It is especially important that you don't forgo these important grooming tasks, though. Keeping your older dog groomed properly can actually head off many problems that now pose greater risk to his health.

Eye Care

Since your Shih Tzu's protruding eyes are so susceptible to injuries, your first step in responsible canine eye care is keeping your dog away from items that pose particular risk. Within the home this may mean getting down to your dog's level—literally. By looking at things from your dog's vantage point, you will likely notice many hazards you would otherwise never see— sharp corners or exposed nails under furniture, for example. Also, keeping your dog's hair out of his face is important, so keep this area trimmed or pull the hair back into an elastic band or ribbon to avoid unnecessary scratching.

Unfortunately, it is not only tangible dangers that threaten your dog's eyes. Medical conditions such as cataracts, glaucoma, and cherry eye can also jeopardise your dog's vision. The best defense? Keeping your own eyes open. By checking your dog's eyes regularly for discharge, redness, cloudiness, or irritation, and seeking veterinary care as needed, you will stack the odds in your dog's favour that any problems will be treatable.

A good habit for eye care is wiping your dog's eyes daily with a soft cloth dipped in distilled water. This will keep the area clean and free of debris, as well as help prevent tearstaining, a common problem in dogs with light-coloured fur. I have found that using an artificial tear solution daily significantly lessens my own dog's eye discharge.

Finally, one of the most important ways of protecting your dog's eyes is bringing him for regular examinations with a veterinary ophthalmologist. Even if your dog's breeding line is free of ocular issues, it is important to remember that any dog can develop degenerative eye diseases. As a breed Shih Tzu are particularly prone to several such conditions.

Dental Care

Keeping your Shih Tzu's teeth clean and healthy not only makes him a more pleasant housemate, it also helps ensure that he will live a long life. Bacteria from dental infections can infiltrate the bloodstream, placing your dog's heart, kidneys, and other organs at an increased risk for countless health problems. If your dog's teeth are already laden with calculus, professional cleaning will be necessary. Ideally, you want to prevent this substance commonly called tartar from forming in the first place. The easiest way to do this? Routine brushing.

Supplies

Similar to shampoo, canine toothpaste differs dramatically from products made for human use. Unlike people, dogs cannot spit toothpaste out after brushing is finished, so it is imperative that you use a brand made specifically for dogs. Many of these are formulated to appeal to the canine palate, and more importantly, they won't make your dog sick.

Although a toothbrush may be helpful, it is not necessary—especially if your dog baulks at the idea of allowing this foreign object into his mouth. A small square of wet gauze wrapped around your index finger can be a very efficient means of cleansing.

FAMILY-FRIENDLY TIP

Everyone Can Play a Part

Involving children in the grooming process is one of the best ways to teach kids about responsible pet care. Even a small child can begin using a brush with supervision. Although you may likely need to go over your dog a second time to ensure a thorough job, allowing your son or daughter to participate will help your Shih Tzu associate a positive feeling with children.

If your preschooler is too young to handle a brush, start by showing how to gently run your fingers through the dog's fur. Especially while your Shih Tzu is a puppy, so much of the grooming process is really about creating the habit and fostering tolerance, not obtaining perfect results. Encouraging your child to participate in all grooming tasks on an age-appropriate level will only help make grooming time a special time for all involved.

A sweater or fleece coat can keep your Shih Tzu warm on a cold day.

The first time you brush your dog's teeth, you may want to use just the gauze and plain water. The next time you can try adding some toothpaste. A slow but steady approach will help your dog see toothbrushing as just another part of his day. He may even enjoy it.

How to Brush Your Shih Tzu's Teeth

Start each toothbrushing session by finding a quiet spot for the task. You may discover that your Shih Tzu feels most comfortable positioned on your lap, or you may both prefer sitting side by side on the floor. The latter option is preferable if your dog flinches once you insert the brush or your finger into his mouth.

Working in an oval pattern, gently begin brushing at a 45-degree angle, directing the brush towards the tartar-prone areas where the teeth meet the gums. Be sure to reach the spaces between the teeth, too. Working on three to four teeth at a time, brush around each set of teeth approximately 10 times, then move on to the next set. The first time you brush, you may only be able to clean your dog's top teeth—or maybe even just the front ones. Don't be discouraged; be dogged. Initially, you may need to revisit the task several times before you are able to finish the job.

Most importantly, don't stop because your dog fusses or wiggles. Instead, continue brushing for a short time period, and always praise him for complying. Depending on his tolerance level, you may be able to continue the task a little longer. It is generally a good idea to end on a positive note.

You should gradually increase the total number of teeth that are cleaned. A reasonable long-term goal is accomplishing two complete brushing sessions each week. Daily sessions are even better! I like to follow up brushing my own dogs' teeth by taking them for their morning walk as soon as we finish. This gives the dogs a fun reward and also helps integrate the task into our daily routine.

Shih Tzu Chic

It is easy to see why so many Shih Tzu owners enjoy embellishing their dogs' looks with fashionable accessories. From hair bows to complete ensembles, the canine attire available today is just plain adorable. For this breed, though, these items are often just as functional as they are aesthetic.

Unless you keep your Shih Tzu's faced trimmed short, bands and bows will be a virtual necessity. You may of course use a simple latex band to keep this hair (referred to as the topknot) out of your dog's eyes, but many owners prefer something more festive. Whatever you use, just be sure not to pull the hair too tightly, or your dog will likely work to remove the item due to discomfort.

Clothing too can be a practical investment for your Shih Tzu if you live in a colder climate. Unlike larger breeds that are barely slowed down by a blizzard, small breeds can be sensitive to much less extreme weather. Fashionable jackets and raingear can help shield your dog from the rain or snow, but on colder days a sweater or fleece coat will definitely keep him warmer. Most are also machine washable.

Is My Puppy Too Young to Visit a Groomer?

The only problem with taking a puppy to the groomer is that he's exposed to a lot of other dogs, both while being groomed and while in the waiting room. To avoid the possibility of infection, you should wait to have your puppy groomed until he's completed all of his puppy vaccinations. These are usually finished when a puppy is around four months old. If you have any questions about how to groom your pup or clip his nails on your own until he's old enough to visit a professional groomer, your vet can advise you.

Chapter 5

Feeling Good

Nothing makes a bigger difference in your Shih Tzu's health than your commitment to this all-important aspect of his life. From the food you serve your beloved companion to the activities you participate in together, you are faced with decisions nearly every day that effect your dog's health. None may be as important, however, as taking your dog for routine veterinary care. The negative effects of countless canine afflictions can be minimised when caught early.

Even conditions once thought of as debilitating are now being easily managed as we learn more and more about these diseases and their causes. As your dog's owner, you are his biggest advocate. As someone who knows canine health, your vet is your best resource.

Finding a Vet

The first step in keeping your Shih Tzu feeling good is establishing a health care regimen. This begins with finding a veterinary practice in your area. Although it is certainly acceptable to travel some distance for a vet you deem worthy of this added time and effort, you will also want to find a more convenient option in case of emergencies. In the UK, vets must offer a 24-hour service. In most cases, the veterinary surgery will use the services of a telephone operator and urgent cases will be directed to an on-call vet. This may be a vet working for several practices or the vets within a practice may share an emergency roster.

When looking for a vet, ask numerous questions, and listen to your instincts as well as the answers. If you get a bad feeling, continue your search. Also, remember that spacious facilities and state of the art technology do not always mean superior service. Some of the best vets are those with smaller waiting rooms that are often packed with clients.

The important factors for you and your dog may be entirely different from another Shih Tzu and his owner. For instance, if your dog seems to tolerate his visits better when he sees the same doctor consistently, you should make sure it is possible to always schedule your appointments with one particular vet. Similarly, some dogs do better in practices that keep their canine and feline clients separate.

Ask for a tour of the practice. Be considerate in terms of scheduling this visit, as the employees cannot provide tours during busier times, but they should be able to fit you in at some point. An unwillingness to let clients view the practice's facilities is a huge red flag. Also, remember that it is not just the vets that will be seeing your dog. Friendly and efficient receptionists and veterinary nurses will also be key in providing your Shih Tzu with the best possible care.

Annual Vet Visits

A skilled vet can make a huge difference in the health of your dog, but this won't be possible unless you bring your dog for his regular appointments. Your Shih Tzu should be seen at least once every year, more often as he gets older. During these routine visits, the vet will check your dog's weight, speak with you about his general behaviour, and address any questions or concerns you may have. The vet should also examine your dog thoroughly and administer any necessary injections for which he is due.

If the practice doesn't mind, it is a good idea to call in with your Shih Tzu at other times throughout the year, as well. Many vets keep treats on hand for this purpose, as it helps animals create positive connotations to visiting the practice. This can have

a huge impact on your dog's reactions to his annual appointments, especially if he is typically frightened or unruly at these times. This is another aspect where the practice's staff plays an impressive role. Caring employees can make the difference between dragging an anxious animal through the doors every 12 months and watching your Shih Tzu happily greet his friends at the vet each time he sees them.

FAMILY-FRIENDLY TIP

Opportunity for Learning

Bringing your baby or toddler along to your Shih Tzu's first vet visit might be difficult—if for no other reason than the physical juggling act of managing both a small child and a nervous dog. A slightly older child, however—say just seven or eight—should be able to tolerate the experience surprisingly well with a little help from you. This early exposure to proper veterinary care can even help teach your child about responsible pet ownership. It may also ease any fears your child may have of visiting his own doctor.

SENIOR DOG TIP

Twice the Prevention

Since many illnesses have a tendency to strike after a dog enters his senior years, it is a wise idea to bring your older Shih Tzu for his routine veterinary examinations every six months instead of annually. This will help your vet diagnose any problems before they become more serious issues.

Vaccinations

Vaccinations have come under a lot of scrutiny in recent years, since research has indicated that administering injections too often can actually harm our pets. While the critics of vaccinating certainly make some valid points, we mustn't overlook the importance of protecting our animals from deadly diseases. In the past, millions of dogs have been killed by infectious diseases, and we owners should think long and hard before rejecting vaccination programmes. The most dangerous diseases for which vaccination is utilised are distemper and parvovirus, and rabies in the US. For younger dogs, any of these can be fatal,

so skipping the vaccination process altogether is simply not the answer. Depending on where you live and what kind of lifestyle you and your dog lead, you may opt to forgo other vaccines that you deem unnecessary. It is vital that any vaccination given to your Shih Tzu is administered at the appropriate age. The most preferable way to determine what is best for your dog is to discuss these issues with your vet and make the decisions together.

Viruses

Canine viruses such as distemper and parvovirus aren't nearly as prevalent as they once were in the UK. Before vaccinations for these illnesses became a part of routine veterinary care, such

Vaccinations have saved the lives of millions of dogs.

After your Shih Tzu's been outside, make sure to check for fleas and ticks.

problems commonly wiped out entire kennels. When modern-day owners fail to vaccinate for these dangerous viruses, even today the likelihood of encountering one of these afflictions increases dramatically, and the results can be just as deadly.

Vaccinations against other serious conditions are also available through most vets. The best way to decide which vaccines your Shih Tzu should receive is to examine your dog's individual circumstances. Talk to your vet and find out about the incidence of disease in your area, and match this information with your dog's individual lifestyle.

Parasites

Though not usually thought of as a dangerous problem, flea bites can lead to a number of serious canine health problems. By protecting your dog with a monthly flea and tick preventative, you can easily avoid a painful and exasperating infestation and possibly several other health issues. In some cases, dogs develop flea allergies that can lead to severe health problems.

Remember that fleas can live in the environment as well as on your dog's body. If you suspect your dog has fleas, treat him and also treat his bedding and the areas of the house he frequents. Ask your vet to recommend a suitable flea treatment for your Shih Tzu and a spray that can be used within the home.

Tick-related Illnesses

Lyme disease has quickly become the most notorious tick-related illness in the US. At the moment, Lyme disease is rare in the UK, but its incidence is increasing. Owners should be aware of the dangers of Lyme disease, and check their dogs for ticks after walking in rural areas.

Why Spay or Neuter?

It's good for your Shih Tzu!
- Spaying and neutering helps dogs live longer, healthier lives
- Spaying and neutering can eliminate or reduce the incidence of a number of health problems that can be very difficult or expensive to treat
- Spaying eliminates the possibility of uterine or ovarian cancer and greatly reduces the incidence of breast cancer, particularly when your pet is spayed before her first estrous cycle
- Neutering eliminates testicular cancer and decreases the incidence of prostate disease

While owners should certainly remain vigilant of the dreaded deer tick, we mustn't overlook the other equally menacing tick varieties that can cause your dog (and your human family members) to become ill. Among the other diseases that ticks can transmit are encephalitis, tulameria, and tick paralysis. Although ticks are very sluggish and incapable of flight, even larger ones can be easily overlooked on a long-haired dog. This is why you should always examine your Shih Tzu thoroughly whenever coming in from the great outdoors.

Removing a Tick

If you find a tick on your dog, use a pair of tweezers to carefully remove it. Since it is vital that you get both the tick's head and body out, your first objective will be getting the tick to simply let go on its own. To do this, use a pair of sterilised tweezers to grasp the tick's body and begin pulling it away from your dog's skin very gently. Apply steady pressure, but be sure not to squeeze too tightly. Jiggling the tick a bit is fine, but don't rotate it.

If you are unable to get the tick to budge after several minutes, apply a drop of alcohol to it. This is often an effective means of getting even the most stubborn tick to release its hold. Once out, drop the tick in a container of alcohol. If the tick will still not release, or if you remove only part of it, seek assistance from your vet.

Breed-specific Illnesses

As in other areas of their lives, all dog breeds have their strengths and weaknesses when it comes to health. Be very wary of any breeder or other caregiver who tells you otherwise. Although some of these conditions can be dangerous, thankfully most are manageable. Of course, not all Shih Tzu will experience the problems associated with their breed, but it helps to know the symptoms so you can ensure the best possible outcome for your dog.

Breathing Difficulties

A common problem among Shih Tzu is a condition called stenotic nares. Caused by abnormally narrow nostrils, stenotic nares restrict normal respiration. A dog suffering from this problem will consequently breathe through his mouth most of the time and wheeze when his mouth is closed. This can be quite disconcerting for owners, who may think their dogs are experiencing an asthmatic attack.

If your dog appears to be having trouble breathing, take him to his vet at once. Upon examination, your vet should be able to diagnose the problem and together with you create a plan to remedy the situation. This may include a surgical procedure called rhinoplasty, which widens the nasal passage, making proper air flow possible.

A common problem among Shih Tzu is a condition called stenotic nares.

Stenotic nares are more common in Shih Tzu and other so-called brachycephalic dogs— that is, those breeds with a short, wide head such as the Pug and Pekingese. Although the condition is usually present at birth, it may not manifest itself for several years.

Heatstroke

Another concern for this short-faced breed is heatstroke. This makes it especially important to watch your Shih Tzu carefully during hot, humid weather. On the most intense days, it is best to keep your dog out of the heat altogether. On milder days, however, keeping an eye on your dog and making lots of drinking water available may be enough to avoid this very serious problem. Perhaps most importantly, remember to never leave your Shih Tzu or any other animal in a parked car. Even during colder weather,

Should You Insure Your Shih Tzu?

Veterinary costs, even for routine procedures, can be expensive—especially if you own more than one pet. Several national companies now offer veterinary health insurance. Similar to human coverage, these policies usually cover emergency care, medication, and the cost of investigating a problem, which may include X-rays, blood tests and ultrasound. Most do not require that you use a specific vet, though, as you will still be paying out of pocket first and then reimbursed for all covered expenses.

If you think such a policy would be helpful in reducing the costs of your dog's veterinary care, talk to your vet to help determine if it's right for you. Your vet should be able to recommend a reputable provider. As with human health insurance, waiting to purchase a policy will only make the premiums more expensive down the road, and possibly even cause denial of coverage for any pre-existing conditions. Right now pet insurance may seem like a luxury, but in the event that your dog needs extensive treatment, it could come in extremely handy in managing the high cost.

the blistering temperatures of a car heater can be just as deadly as those caused by the summer sun.

Eye Problems

Because the Shih Tzu's eyes naturally protrude, this breed is also more vulnerable to a number of eye injuries. Often these can result in a problem called a corneal ulcer. When an ulcer forms, it is both painful and itchy, often causing your dog to rub the area and worsen the problem. Corneal ulcers may also form as a result of bacteria or fungal infection.

Most common in young and active dogs, eye ulcers are graded according to their depth, which can vary. Prevention is ideal. Keeping your home free of possible dangers is one of the best ways to prevent accidents from happening, but don't forget to be aware of your Shih Tzu's surroundings when he is away from home, as well. If you take your dog for walks in the woods, for instance, keep the lead short, so you can help him avoid any protruding sticks or other hazards lurking in his path. When this is not possible, treatments may range from antibiotic ointments for superficial ulcers to various forms of surgical repair for more complicated situations.

Another common problem among Shih Tzu is prolapsed gland of the third eyelid. This condition, nicknamed cherry eye for the unsightly red mass protruding from the corner of the dog's eye, can be quite alarming for an inexperienced or squeamish owner. Fortunately, it looks much

Generally, Shih Tzu are a healthy breed.

worse than it feels, but irritation and infection can occur if cherry eye is left untreated. Like ulcerations, this condition can be caused by an injury or may appear without any physical trauma whatsoever. Frequently surgery is necessary, but in minor cases steroids are sufficient for reducing swelling.

Hypothyroidism

Since it doesn't take much of an increase for smaller breeds to reach obesity, your Shih Tzu may become heavier than you'd like before you realise that his weight is a problem. If your dog's food intake or lack of exercise is clearly the cause, a diet and exercise plan may be all that's needed to reverse the situation. If, however, you notice an increase in weight for no apparent reason, you should ask your vet if hypothyroidism could be the explanation.

In addition to weight gain, dry skin and hair loss are also signs of this endocrine disorder. When the thyroid gland is underactive, your dog's metabolism decreases, making it easier for him to gain weight. The typical age of onset is between 4 and 10 years. Once a diagnosis has been made, treatment with a synthetic thyroid hormone is usually used. Although periodic blood samples should be taken to ensure proper treatment, the condition is generally highly manageable.

Kidney Failure (Renal Dysplasia and Hypoplasia)

About a year ago, I received an e-mail from a friend of mine who told me that her seven-year-old Shih Tzu, Charlie, had passed away unexpectedly due to kidney failure. Knowing that I specialised in writing about animal

A dog with patellar luxation will appear lame for no apparent reason.

health and behaviour, she asked me what she could do to prevent this tragic outcome for her other two dogs, particularly Charlie's son. Was the condition hereditary? Common in Shih Tzu? The answer to both these questions was a qualified yes.

Kidney failure can occur for a variety of reasons, ranging from antifreeze poisoning or infection to tumours or dehydration. Renal hypoplasia and renal dysplasia, however, is specifically associated with underdeveloped or abnormally formed kidneys, and it is more common in Shih Tzu than many other breeds. It is also genetic. Dogs suffering from this condition usually reach the state of kidney failure at a much earlier age than those whose kidney functioning deteriorates for other reasons.

Symptoms of renal hypoplasia include excessive water intake, overly frequent urination, vomiting, and diarrhoea. These signs usually appear between six months and two years of age, but unfortunately, by the time they do, the kidneys are already at least 70-percent destroyed. Prevention is always the best form of treatment, but preventing a hereditary affliction such as this can be especially problematic. This is why you should ask a breeder what kind of genetic testing has been done on his or her dogs.

A good safety precaution—especially if you know little about your dog's family tree—is having your vet run routine urine and blood analysis tests, so a problem can be diagnosed before it is too late. Specialised diets (containing lower amounts of protein) are often helpful in managing this condition. Although the disease is not reversible, when a dog is diagnosed before symptoms appear, he has a significantly better chance of living a longer, more comfortable life.

Patellar Luxation

As your Shih Tzu's leg bends and straightens normally, his patella (the technical term for the kneecap) slides up and down within a groove in his femur. When the kneecap slips out of this groove, it is called patellar luxation. The causes for this problem can vary and may include such possibilities as a malformation of the groove itself.

Luxation, or dislocation, may happen over and over or it might only happen occasionally, so treatment will depend on the intensity of the problem. If the problem is only intermittent, it may require only a simple adjustment by your vet. If luxation is chronically repetitive, however, surgery may be necessary. Osteoarthritis can also develop over time if the condition persists.

Your Shih Tzu's First Aid Kit

The following items should always be kept on hand in the event of a medical emergency:

- Antibiotic ointment
- Canine first-aid manual
- Children's diphenhydramine (antihistamine)
- Cotton buds
- Emergency phone numbers
- Torch
- Hydrogen peroxide
- Instant ice pack
- Ipecac syrup
- Nonstick gauze pads, gauze, and tape
- Oral syringe or eyedropper
- Rectal thermometer
- Saline solution
- Scissors
- Soap
- Styptic powder or pencil
- Tweezers
- Any other item your vet recommends keeping on hand

Remember to keep an eye on expiration dates and throw away any products when they should no longer be used.

More common in smaller breeds, patellar luxation is relatively easy to spot and usually manifests itself by the time a dog is six months old. A dog with this problem will appear lame for no apparent reason— or merely hop for a few steps at a time if the problem is a sporadic one. Although surgical prognosis can vary, most dogs return to full function providing that activity is properly limited during the recovery period.

Yearly checkups are the best way to ensure a lifetime of good health for your Shih Tzu.

Shih Tzu

General Illnesses

Cancer

No one likes to hear the word cancer. Being told that your dog has a malignancy can be devastating. What it doesn't have to be, however, is a death sentence. Mast cell tumours, one of the most common forms of canine cancer, can frequently be removed with an excellent prognosis. Fortunately, the Shih Tzu is not one of the breeds prone to cancer, but any dog can be faced with this disease.

Early detection of cancer, perhaps more so than any other affliction, is crucial. By checking your dog frequently for any suspicious lumps or bumps, you increase his chances of beating this brutal disease. If you do notice any abnormalities, notify your dog's vet immediately. It is important to note, however, that not all cancers present themselves in obvious ways, so be sure to keep an eye on your dog's overall health and behaviour in addition to being on the lookout for unusual growths.

One of the best ways of preventing your Shih Tzu from being diagnosed with cancer is spaying or neutering your dog early. Spaying your female puppy will prevent her from being stricken with ovarian cancer, and it may significantly lessen her risk for mammary tumours, as well. Neutering your male Shih Tzu will similarly prevent testicular cancer.

Epilepsy

Witnessing a canine seizure can be extremely scary for an unsuspecting owner, but there is usually no way to predict if or when your dog will experience this kind of incident. A fitting animal may shake, appear dizzy, or even fall from his feet. In some instances there is a loss of bladder or bowel control, as well. As hard as it may sound, the best thing you can do for your dog in this situation is remain calm. In fact, by paying close attention to the circumstances surrounding the seizure, you may be able to help avert a future attack.

Not all dogs that experience a seizure are necessarily suffering from epilepsy. Fitting can also be a symptom of several other conditions, including allergies, low blood sugar (hypoglycemia), or occasionally even more serious problems such as tumours. It is very important that you report a seizure to your dog's vet for this reason.

If the problem is indeed epilepsy, there are several approaches a vet may take. In many cases medical treatment is not even necessary. If the seizures occur too frequently, for long periods of time (a seizure lasting more than a minute or two is considered significant), or if the episodes are extremely intense, an anticonvulsant medication may be prescribed. When not a secondary problem, most canine seizures will not prevent a dog from living an otherwise normal life.

Complementary Therapies

At one time many ancient forms of medicine—including acupuncture, homeopathy, and other Eastern practices—were grouped together under the umbrella term *alternative medicine*. Although the premise of these modalities is indeed quite different from more conventional Western techniques, the word alternative is actually a bit misleading, implying that the two ways are mutually exclusive. The truth is that these different approaches can often work together for a more comprehensive plan for your pet. Many contemporary vets therefore prefer the term *complementary medicine*.

What Is a Holistic Vet?

Most of us have heard the term *holistic medicine*, but what does it mean? A holistic vet approaches your dog in a way that encompasses his entire being—his physical health, as well as his mental and emotional condition. (The word holistic actually means *whole*.) Often utilising such ancient practices as acupuncture and homeopathy, holistic vets think it is vital to evaluate all circumstances surrounding an animal's problem. This can understandably be a lengthy process with many questions requiring thoughtful answers.

Feeling Good

Acupuncture

Acupuncture, the process of using fine needles to stimulate energy and recovery in the body, has been shown to help with issues such as allergies, skin problems, arthritis, and even cancer. It can also be remarkably effective for dogs that have experienced musculoskeletal problems. Although the concept of inserting needles into the body may sound painful, countless owners have witnessed their pets dozing off during treatment sessions—and more importantly, a significant number also report marked improvement after several visits.

Homeopathy

Homeopathy, another ancient modality, combats illnesses by using the substances that caused these sicknesses in the first place. Sound confusing? Believe it or not, this is very similar to the way vaccination works. By introducing highly diluted doses of these problem-causing substances into your dog's body, homeopathy works to create a natural immunity. By allowing your Shih Tzu to be exposed to this infinitesimal amount of a particular agent, you are consequently helping him to create antibodies that will work even harder when confronted with this same substance in the future.

An inexperienced caregiver should never apply the science of homeopathy. Although the amounts of the substances used are indeed minute—far less than those employed in most vaccines—one of the most basic premises of homeopathy is that smaller doses can be astonishingly powerful. Many practitioners even insist that the smaller the dose, the more intense the effect.

Chiropractic Care and Physical Therapy

Other forms of complementary medicine include chiropractic care and physical therapy. Although both of these methods are quite common in the realm of human medicine, they are still quite new to many pet owners. Like acupuncture and homeopathy, both of these have been utilised for treating a variety of injuries for many years.

Finding a Qualified Vet

Anyone providing your Shih Tzu with any kind of veterinary care should be trained and certified by an appropriate organisation, such as the British Association of Veterinary Homeopathy, for example. You may find that your own vet is certified by one of the specialist organisations, but never assume that just because a person is a licensed vet that he or she is qualified to perform complementary medicine.

As with any kind of treatment, outcomes can vary by individual. Your Shih Tzu may experience great success with one form of complementary medicine, but not so much with another. Likewise, one dog might not benefit from a specific modality that had a remarkable effect on another. Results can also take time, so be patient as well as discerning when evaluating a particular method.

Coping With a Veteran's Declining Health

One of the hardest parts of pet ownership is watching our canine friends get older. With the geriatric years there come a number of common afflictions, such as arthritis, greater vulnerability to injury, and even depression. The best way you can help your older Shih Tzu enjoy his golden years is to make preventive care a part of his life from the very beginning. Dogs that are fed nutritious food, given adequate exercise, and brought for routine veterinary visits stand a far greater chance at beating everything from the blues to cancer. Like all of us, our canine companions must age, but dogs are now living considerably longer than in years past, and we are constantly learning new ways to make their senior years quality ones.

Chapter 6

Being Good

Although Shih Tzu are smaller than most other breeds, they are definitely no less canine because of the size difference. This petite dog can do nearly all the things a larger dog can, and he is prone to the same unpleasant behaviours if not properly trained. In some cases these negative behaviours can become even more deeply ingrained in a small breed, because many owners think that, like their dogs, these problems are tiny. After all, an aggressive Shih Tzu can't really hurt anyone, right? Wrong!

A Shih Tzu, like every other dog, must be respected, and the best way to do so is by teaching him proper behaviour.

Training can begin as early as the day you bring your Shih Tzu home. You may limit yourself to one type of training at a time—waiting until your dog has mastered housetraining, for example, before moving on to teaching obedience commands. Or you may do both simultaneously. While patience will take you far, you should never give up on your dog—or think that he is any less capable of learning because of his size. When it comes to learning, these wise little dogs have big potential.

Finding a Trainer

Finding a dog trainer is easy; finding a *good* trainer can also be easy, but it requires a little extra effort and sometimes a bit of patience, as well. First, you must identify your goals. Certainly, you may begin by wanting to teach your Shih Tzu just a few basic commands, and you might later decide that your dog has an aptitude for competitive obedience. But if you know from the beginning that this is your objective, you should seek a trainer with experience in the ring.

Speaking with other owners involved in the pastime can often yield valuable recommendations—either towards good trainers or away from the less desirable ones. Other resources for referrals are your vet, or you can talk to your dog-owning friends in your area and find out where they train. The Kennel Club lists local training clubs.

Just because you don't plan to enter

your dog in obedience, this doesn't mean that your standards should be lower. Perhaps you are seeking a trainer to help with a specific problem, or maybe your dog is a slower learner or just a little skittish. It is especially important that you find a trainer who understands how to best deal with your dog's individual personality. Beware of anyone who insists that a single approach works equally well for all dogs.

Finally, listen to your instincts and watch for your dog's reactions, too. Animals are extremely good judges of character. If you have a bad feeling, heed it. If your dog backs it up, there should be no question that it is time to seek a new trainer.

Socialisation

Most Shih Tzu love people. When the only individuals a dog is regularly exposed to are his family members, however, his natural tendency to welcome interactions with new people can dwindle. His temperament may even become aggressively overprotective

Crates aren't tiny jails! They are safe places for your Shih Tzu to relax.

of those he loves—a dangerous albeit well intended shift in behaviour. Perhaps your dog would never bite anyone, but he barks virtually nonstop whenever company arrives or if he encounters another dog at the park. Wherever your Shih Tzu falls on the socialisation scale, one thing is certain—frequent positive experience with other pets, children, and people will only serve to make him more delightful than he already is.

Because your dog is smaller than most of the other dogs he encounters, it is particularly important that he not be antagonistic in the presence of other animals. It is also imperative that your dog is affable in the presence of children. Certainly, a dog should never be left alone with a child (for both their sakes), but even if a child approaches your dog rather abruptly, you could still face a steep fine (or worse) if he bites in reaction.

On a more private level, it is a widely held theory that what dogs want most is the company of other dogs, so allowing your Shih Tzu to experience positive exchanges with other members of his species may likely be a means of fulfilling a basic canine need—much like our own need for fellow

Beware of Over-pampering!

There is nothing wrong with pampering your Shih Tzu. Every dog needs to be loved and protected by his owner, and there are indeed special precautions owners of small breeds must take—not leaving your dog alone with larger, more aggressive breeds, for example. The diminutive size of the Shih Tzu, though, can give some owners the impression that these little dogs need to be treated differently from other dogs. This is simply not the case. Your Shih Tzu does not need to be carried everywhere—he enjoys walking just as much as the next dog. Normal running and playful interaction with friendly dogs his own size (or even a bit bigger) is also good exercise for him.

When an owner moves from pampering his pooch with love and affection (and an occasional new toy or other treat) to tolerating unacceptable behaviours—such as growling or biting—it is no longer a matter of simple indulgence. There's a reason it is called spoiling!

Socialise your puppy from the moment you bring him home, encouraging friends and neighbours to be the ones handing out the treats at times. Remember that small dogs can be aggressive, too—especially if they are allowed to believe they are in charge.

human companionship. The Basset Hound who lives across the street may be just another dog to you, but to your Shih Tzu he might be the closest thing to a friend just like himself.

Help your dog build positive connotations of people by supplying friends and friendly strangers with treats to offer him in social situations. When a stranger asks if he or she may pet your Shih Tzu, say yes, and praise your dog excitedly for a pleasant response. Soon he will welcome this kind of interaction.

The great thing about socialising your Shih Tzu is that it's such an easy task. Simply bring your dog along with you whenever you are going

somewhere that he may go as well. If you are a homebody, this may mean making the effort to get out each day—even if just for a walk around your neighbourhood. But you just might find that getting out is fun for both of you.

Crate Training

If you plan to travel with your Shih Tzu, crate training will be extremely useful. In the US, this may well mean plane travel. In the UK, most owners are content to have good car travellers. Crate training is also extremely practical even if you do *not* plan to take your dog along with you on trips, as the kennels used by many boarding facilities are extremely similar in structure to a crate. By making sure your dog is comfortable inside a crate, you are creating a portable environment that can keep your dog safe no matter where he goes.

Especially while your Shih Tzu is young and more prone to mischief, using a crate when you cannot properly supervise him may be the smartest option for both of you. It can save your home and other possessions from being ruined, and it can save your dog from getting seriously hurt. Although you may no longer need to use the crate as frequently as your dog enters adulthood, you may likely find that he still seeks out this place of refuge for naps and as a spot to hide or enjoy special treats.

Many Shih Tzu sleep alongside their owners in their beds, but the crate is often a safer place for them. (If being away from your dog at night bothers you, consider keeping his crate in your bedroom or moving it there at bedtime.) Especially while housetraining your dog, you may find this is the best way to make sure you don't awake to an unpleasant surprise atop your duvet. In multi-dog households some owners even prefer to use the crate as a location for feeding time to help ensure that each dog is eating his own food or getting his fair share.

Don't Force it

Of course, some dogs simply don't take to crate training. A rescued Shih Tzu may have a deep-rooted fear or some other kind of anxiety regarding crates, as he many have been crated for excessively long periods. With patience, you may be able to teach your rescued Shih Tzu that his crate is a safe, cosy den rather than a cage he cannot escape from. But if your

Help your dog become socialised by exposing him to gentle, friendly children.

Shih Tzu is seriously concerned, it is best to skip the crating process altogether.

How to Crate Train

The first rule of crate training is that the crate must never be used for punishment. It should also never be used for more than a few hours at a time. Begin by placing the crate in its designated location in your home with the door wide open. Your Shih Tzu will notice it straight away and may enter all on his own to investigate his new surroundings.

You may also encourage your dog to check out his crate by placing a toy or treat inside, but don't rush to close the door right away. Once your dog seems comfortable being inside the crate, you can then start closing the door for very short periods of time, gradually increasing the length and ultimately leaving the room. Praise your dog whenever he enters, and try to always end on a positive note. Even if he howls wildly when you first close the door, wait for that one or two seconds he is quiet to re-open it—and again, praise him lavishly.

Housetraining

Sometimes referred to as housebreaking, housetraining is one of the most important tasks you will undertake with your Shih Tzu puppy. Although it may seem like an insurmountable goal in the very

Never punish your Shih Tzu for housetraining mistakes.

beginning, persistence will indeed pay off in the end. The best tool at your disposal is perhaps the simplest one—a schedule. By keeping track of the times your dog is eating and drinking, you can more easily predict when toileting time is near. (When my own dogs were housetraining, I even went so far as to keep a chart on my refrigerator to keep track of all the details, including the most common times for accidents, so I could hopefully avoid them in the future.)

An eight-week-old puppy will need to eliminate once every two hours. Take heart, though, as this menacingly short interval will increase as he gets just a little older. By the time your Shih Tzu is just four months old, he should only need to visit his toilet spot every four hours. Dogs learn at different paces, but providing you afford him ample opportunity and praise him lavishly whenever he goes in the correct spot, your dog may even be reliably housetrained by this time.

The One-minute Warning

In addition to common times for accidents, you may notice that your dog also offers you telltale signs that he is ready to void his bladder or bowels. Though the signal can differ from dog to dog, most pups do have some sort of ritual that they perform when this time comes. Some dogs walk in a circle; others pace back and forth. Maybe your Shih Tzu sniffs around him. I call this the one-minute warning, because if you do not get your dog to the proper place quickly once this sign is shown, you will almost certainly be cleaning up an accident.

Using the Crate

If you have chosen to provide your dog with a crate, this will be also be an invaluable tool in the housetraining process—for the simple reason that a dog prefers not to soil his personal space. By keeping your puppy crated when you cannot keep a close eye on him, you lower the risk of his urinating or defaecating inside your home and increase the risk of his learning the correct place for elimination.

Again, if your dog came from a rescue centre and was crated for long periods in a previous home, he may not mind the presence of excrement in his crate for the simple reason that he was once forced to use this space as a makeshift bathroom. In this case it is best to use a baby gate to stop your dog relieving himself on rugs and other difficult to clean areas of your home.

Accidents Happen

Always remove your dog from visual range while you wash the floor or carpet after an accident. Allowing him to watch can inadvertently give him the impression that his job is to make the mess and your job is to clean it. If you are using a crate, this can be an ideal place for your dog at this time, but make sure you let your dog return to the room once the cleanup is

Treats for Training

When using food as a training tool, remember to offer bite-sized portions that can be quickly consumed. If it takes too long to chew the treat, your Shih Tzu may become distracted from the task on which you are working. Some owners might also find that it helps to use different treats for training sessions than for other more casual moments. Your dog may likely work harder for tasty cubes of grilled chicken, for example, than for the same dog biscuits he knows he will likely get when he returns from his walk later that day.

Oops!

Expect your puppy to have a few accidents in the house—
it's a normal part of housetraining. Here's what to do when
that happens:

- When you catch him in the act of relieving himself in the house,
  do something to interrupt him, like make a startling noise (be careful
  not to scare him). Immediately take him to his toilet spot, praise him, and
  give him a treat if he finishes relieving himself there.
- Don't punish your puppy for toiletting in the house. If you find a soiled area,
  it's too late to administer a correction. Just clean it up. Rubbing your puppy's
  nose in it, taking him to the spot and scolding him, or any other punishment
  will only make him afraid of you or afraid to relieve himself in your presence.
  In fact, punishment will often do more harm than good.
- Cleaning the soiled area is very important because puppies are highly
  motivated to continue soiling in areas that smell like urine or faeces.
- It's extremely important that you use the supervision and confinement
  procedures outlined above to prevent the number of accidents. If you allow your
  puppy to relieve himself frequently in the house, he'll get confused about where
  he's supposed to relieve himself, which will prolong the housetraining process.

done—and *never* give the impression that you are banishing him to the crate for what he has done.

The easiest way to ensure that your dog will not revisit the scene of the crime is to properly clean the area. This means not only absorbing all the wetness and thoroughly washing the area, but also spraying it with an odour-eliminating cleaner. Several products of this kind are available at most pet supply stores; some are even available in the form of convenient wipes. Avoid products that use ammonia, though, as this is an inherent ingredient of urine and therefore an agent likely to actually inspire a repeat offense.

Like children, animals respond better to praise than punishment. For this reason I highly recommend focusing on the times your dog relieves himself in the proper place—and ignoring the accidents. I assure you that yelling at your Shih Tzu, striking him with a newspaper (or your hand), or rubbing his nose in excrement will do nothing to help housetrain him. These abusive acts will only frighten your dog and likely ruin your relationship with him.

Basic Commands

When it comes to training, consistency matters much more than the length of each session; therefore, make training a regular but short part of every day. In the very beginning, limit the time you spend teaching a particular command to around five minutes. As your dog gets used to the training process, gradually increase this period by five minutes at a time, with an ultimate goal of 15-minute sessions. If your dog seems open to spending more time on a particular command or task, increase the number of sessions each day as opposed to the duration of these periods. Training your Shih Tzu should be a fun process for both you and your dog, so always be watchful of signs that your dog is losing his focus. If he seems distracted or tired, it may be time to call it a day.

While it demands a serious commitment on behalf of the owner, training a dog does not require a great deal of expense. Most basic training classes are surprisingly economical. You may even find that your Shih Tzu can learn virtually any command in your own garden once you have learned the proper training techniques. There are countless books and videos available to assist you with this task. Basic dog training also requires very little in the way of equipment. A

simple lead and a pocketful of bite-sized treats will take you both far. One of the most effective tools of the trade—a clicker—can be found at pet stores very inexpensively. Though not a necessity, this simple plastic noisemaker works by conditioning your dog and is one of the best ways to reinforce his training success.

Sit

I recommend teaching the *sit* command before any others, because it is truly a hands-on experience for owners and tends to be an easily mastered task for most dogs. Simply hold the treat up over your dog's nose and slowly move it back over his head as you issue the command, "Sit." Most dogs will naturally move into the sitting position when this is done. You may then give him the treat, but don't forget to utter an enthusiastic *good boy*. Though edible rewards can be extremely effective for training, they cannot replace the power of praise.

Come

I am also a huge advocate of teaching dogs the *come* command. Maybe you don't think your Shih Tzu needs to learn a full array of obedience

It's a good idea to teach sit first, since it is easily mastered by most dogs.

commands, and you're right, if that's what you think is best for you and your dog. Teaching this one word, however, can literally save your dog's life. If your Shih Tzu ever gets away from you, having successfully taught this single command is like having an invisible lead at your disposal.

The best way to teach this command is by catching your dog already in the act of coming to you. Whenever you see your Shih Tzu moving your way, say the word *come* in an upbeat tone, and praise him lavishly for doing so. Soon he will begin to associate the word with the action. You can work with your dog in any safe environment—a fenced garden or a large, open family room, for example. You can also practice with your dog on an extendable lead nearly anywhere. If working off-lead, just be sure to have a friend help you, as it is especially important that you have a way of making your dog comply with the command. Most importantly, never admonish your dog for coming when called—if he has done something unpleasant, for instance. Your dog should never fear coming to you.

Stay

The *stay* command is best taught once your dog has mastered sitting. After issuing the *sit* command, raise your hand and say the word *stay* as you back up very slowly. In the beginning, your Shih Tzu may only remain still for a few seconds, but it is especially important to offer praise during this time, however short.

Gradually increase the number of steps you take away from your dog. You should also increase the amount of time before you offer praise or a reward. Eventually, your Shih Tzu should be able to stay for about a minute or longer with you at least 10 feet away.

Down

Teaching the *down* command is most easily accomplished by using an edible reward. With your dog in a sitting position, issue the command while lowering the treat in front of him. Most dogs will naturally lower their bodies to get the treat, but if your dog does not, try slowly pulling the treat away from him. You can also draw your dog downward.

Since your Shih Tzu is already positioned so close to the floor, lowering the treat may be a very subtle

Make teaching down easy by using a yummy food reward.

gesture. If your find this difficult, start by simply pulling the treat away from him or drawing him downward while saying the word *down*. Eventually, you should start issuing the command before even bringing out the reward, as you do not want your dog's compliance to be dependent on the physical motion of lowering the treat.

Heel

Although your Shih Tzu is not likely to be pulling you to your feet if he doesn't learn how to walk properly on a lead, he *can* injure himself if he is allowed to pull incessantly whenever you take him for a walk. Teaching the *heel* command can help with this.

This is another command for which the *sit* command is a prerequisite. Begin by walking your dog on your left side with the lead in your right hand and a treat in your left. When you stop, say the word *sit*. When he complies, reward him and say the word *heel*. Then begin walking again, stopping periodically to practice this two-part exercise. Your ultimate goal is for your dog to comfortably walk alongside you, stopping whenever you do. The *heel* command will be particularly useful if you plan to involve your Shih Tzu in formal obedience.

Tricks

Many Shih Tzu are natural goofballs. They seem to truly love entertaining their owners with their lively antics. This intelligent breed is also highly capable of learning more structured tricks. From shaking hands to rolling

FAMILY-FRIENDLY TIP

Help Wanted

Involving kids in the training process can be a positive experience for all involved. Still, safety (both your child's and your dog's) should always top the priority list. For a small child this may mean that her job is merely to join you in praising your Shih Tzu when he does well. This allows her to feel part of the process while at the same time learning how to gently interact with your dog by observing you.

Older kids can take on more responsibility in the training process, but it is especially important to teach a child not to un-do what you have already done. For example, if you are in the process of training your dog to walk on a lead, your child must know how to continue with this training before letting her hold the lead. Even a small dog can often take a child for a walk instead of the other way around, and it doesn't take long for the new behaviour to become ingrained. Also, it is particularly important to teach your child not to let your dog gnaw on her hand. Even when done playfully, this can inadvertently teach your Shih Tzu that biting and chewing are acceptable behaviours.

Being Good

SENIOR DOG TIP

Training the Older Dog

If you are adopting an older dog, you may not need to spend as much time on the basic forms of training. Many older dogs, for example, will have little interest in chewing shoes or furniture (or even their own toys), since they completed the teething process long before arriving in their new homes. Still, you might find that your Shih Tzu's previous owner never taught him how to properly walk on a lead or that growling over food is unacceptable. Some remedial housetraining may be necessary due to the stress of your dog's transition from one home to another.

The old saying *you can't teach an old dog new tricks* simply isn't true. Older dogs can be just as capable of being trained as younger ones. They may, however, need a little extra time and patience along the way. Just as human senior citizens get bored without meaningful activities in their lives, so do older dogs. Continuing to play and interact with your senior Shih Tzu will even help him reach his learning potential, as keeping mentally fit helps pave the way for all future learning.

over, many owners insist there is nothing a Shih Tzu cannot do.

I remember watching my grandparents' Shih Tzu, Tammy (they named her after me), dancing all around their kitchen floor on just her hind legs when I was a teenager. Most often she did this for a special treat—lettuce and raw green beans were her favourites. She would often do this even when no one was offering her food. I remember thinking at the time that she was the most playful dog I had ever met. I spent hours on that kitchen floor playing with her, or was she amusing me? I think the line was indeed a fine one.

By using the techniques of food rewards described in this chapter, you can teach your Shih Tzu virtually any dog trick. Just be sure to offer both your praise and the edible reward while your dog is still in the process of performing the trick. If you are trying to teach your dog to shake hands, for example, you should provide the reward while your Shih Tzu's paw is still in your hand. Begin by holding his paw up and shaking it gently as you tell him to *shake hands* (or whatever words you choose for the command). It is fine to praise this early level of success when he complies, but it will take him longer to equate the reward with the task if you offer the treat once his paw returns to the floor or ground. You can even make up your own tricks. One of the best things about these generous little spirits is their willingness to learn—and to teach us in the process.

What *Is* He Saying?

For many years animal experts have analysed the ways in which dogs *speak* to humans through body language. Most of us are familiar with the better known examples of this unspoken communication—a happily wagging tail, the bottoms-up position aptly named a "playbow," and even the tail between the legs stance that has evolved into a figurative way for humans to describe a frightened person. But did you know that dogs may be speaking to us in other ways, as well?

I recently interviewed a woman named Monica Diedrich who works worldwide as an animal communicator. Describing herself as an interpreter for animals and their human companions, she frequently visits with families who are experiencing behaviour problems within their households. Part of her job is to tell these people why their dogs are behaving in the ways they are and to help their owners solve these problems.

Although work in cross-species communication is gaining popularity among pet owners, it still draws its share of sceptics. Whether you think it is possible for animal communicators like Diedrich to converse with dogs or not, here is something she told me that is definitely worth considering: When our animals misbehave, they are often trying to tell us something—much like a child may sometimes act out in an attempt to capture the parents' attention. A dog that is left at home alone all day, for example, may decide the best way to express his

Shih Tzu's love to entertain with their lively antics.

dissatisfaction with the arrangement is to chew all his master's belongings. This is perhaps an obvious example, but one that nevertheless illustrates the point.

I believe there are countless ways in which our dogs try to communicate with us. As caring and responsible owners, it is our job to learn how to interpret what they are saying. For some this is as simple as just looking into their dogs' eyes. For others it may take a little more time, but if we open our hearts and minds, we just might find that continuing to listen can lead us to a better understanding of both our dogs and ourselves.

Being Good

Chapter 7

In the

Doghouse

One of the most important traits of any dog owner is patience. Many dog-training tasks take time. Housetraining, for example, may come easily for one Shih Tzu, but it might take another several weeks or months before he becomes completely reliable. Providing a loving and supportive environment is key in helping your dog master any milestone. Owners should not, however, be so patient that they ignore serious problems such as chronic housesoiling, excessive barking, or destructive behaviours.

Problems like excessive barking may be a result of boredom or loneliness.

trainer or animal behaviourist. If you have been working with your Shih Tzu to no avail (or with only marginal success), ask your vet for an opinion. Sometimes all it takes is a fresh perspective. Your vet may be able to pinpoint the one key strategy you may be overlooking, or he or she might validate your suspicion that it's time to seek help from a professional.

If your dog is placing himself or other household members in danger by his behaviour, however, the answer is clear: You need help fast. Your vet is still one of your best resources in this situation, but you may also seek referrals from your local rescue centre. You can also get information from the Association of Pet Behaviour Counsellors by logging on to their website: www.apbc.org.uk..

Barking (Excessive)

Like housesoiling, excessive barking can sometimes be caused by legitimate reasons. If your dog is left alone for long periods of time, he may turn

W hen these kinds of issues present themselves, owners should certainly respond with that same level of love and support, but they also must take action. Ignoring any problem will only make it worse.

Is it Really a Problem?

Sometimes it's hard to know whether a problem requires the help of a

to barking or howling as a means of coping with his loneliness. Or your dog might be barking in response to various sounds he hears. Just because you can pinpoint the cause of your dog's barking, however, does not make it acceptable. In addition to your own distaste of the constant noise, anyone within earshot of your dog at these times likely finds his barking just as unpleasant as you do.

Barking on Command

When my breeder told me the best way to deal with excessive barking, I couldn't help but laugh. "Before you can teach a dog *not to* bark," she seriously instructed, "you must first teach him how *to* bark." Show me the dog that needs to be taught how to bark, I instantly thought. But the more she explained her point, the more sense it made to me. Think about it. Your dog probably already knows how to bark—obviously—but does he bark on command? Interestingly, teaching your dog to speak is central in getting him to understand the difference between barking and not barking.

My breeder suggests starting by making a particular sound—knocking on a table, for example, and issuing the command *speak*. If your dog is anything like mine, doing this will instantly elicit a barking frenzy. The next step is a little more difficult, though. You must begin rewarding the dog as soon as he stops barking. Now you may counter that your dog never stops barking, that this is in fact the problem. If you listen carefully, though, you will notice brief pauses in between your dog's vocalisations. It is at one of these very short instances that the reward must come.

In some cases a simple *good boy* following the command *enough* may be sufficient for reinforcing the silence. More likely, though, you will

Finding a Behaviourist

Since animal behaviourists do not currently need any form of licensing to do their work, dog owners must be very careful when selecting someone to help with their dogs' behaviour problems. Your local phone book may be filled with people who specialise in this field involving the observation, interpretation, and modification of animal behaviour, but it is very important to make sure the person you choose is qualified. Most professional behaviourists come from a background in psychology and are certified through the International Association of Pet Behaviour Counsellors. Ideally, you want a person with a certain level of education and experience dealing with animals, particularly small breeds. Dog training knowledge and experience are also desirable.

need to provide your dog with a more tangible reward, such as a small, easy to swallow treat. My breeder also recommends using a clicker. This small, inexpensive noisemaking device can be found at most pet supply stores and works by conditioning your Shih Tzu to associate the sound of the clicker with whatever behaviour is present at the time of the click. For this reason it is especially important that you use the clicker at precisely the right moment.

Other Solutions

If loneliness is the culprit, employing a pet sitter may be the answer. If outside commotion tends to trigger barking, consider moving your dog's crate into a quieter room of your home and leaving the radio or television turned on whenever you leave. Even the littlest dogs often believe it is their duty to protect their human family members, and this instinct can be very deeply ingrained. Perhaps you even want your Shih Tzu to act as a watchdog. If this is the case, just be sure to help your dog understand that his job is to bring suspicious noises to your attention and

then let you decide what to do from there. The *enough* command is usually the best means of doing this.

Chewing

Some dogs are definitely worse chewers than others. One might not suspect that a Shih Tzu could destroy a pair of fine leather shoes in five minutes flat, but these tiny dogs have amazingly powerful little teeth and jaws. A dog's breed actually has little to do with it. Your first Shih Tzu may leave his teething habits behind with puppyhood, but your second might have an insatiable hunger for everything inedible well into his adult years.

Solutions

The best defense, as the saying goes, is a good offense. Start by removing any tempting items from your dog's reach. This means putting away things like shoes, books, toys—basically anything that may normally find its way onto the floor. Of course, some items cannot be

Puppies need to chew, so give your dog plenty of safe chew toys.

as easily removed from your dog's path—furniture, for example. In the case that your dog shows an interest in chewing these items, you will need to create a distraction or a deterrent.

Digging is a natural behaviour for dogs.

Many times a simple distraction is enough to divert your Shih Tzu's attention away from the unacceptable item. By redirecting your dog to his Nylabone when he starts chewing your coffee table's leg, you teach him that his things are okay for chewing, but yours are not. Refrain from offering your old (or chewed) items as toys for your dog. Although these objects may have surpassed their usefulness to you, your dog will probably have a hard time distinguishing between the old item you no longer want and a newer replacement item that you do not want destroyed.

If your dog appears to be seeking out a particular item for his chewing enjoyment, a good way of dissuading him is treating the item with a non-toxic substance made especially for discouraging chewing. These bitter-tasting products effectively take the fun out of chewing certain items. Be sure to read the label carefully before applying these sprays to fabric or other items that may become stained from their use, though.

Digging

There are many different reasons a dog may dig. If you can identify your dog's reason, there is a good chance you will be able to improve the situation. Your Shih Tzu may dig a hole in your garden to stay cool on a hot day. On a completely different level, your dog may be digging because he is suffering from separation anxiety. Or your dog may dig out of boredom or simple curiosity. Frequently, dogs kept fenced inside small spaces will dig to escape these boundaries. Unfortunately, digging is also a natural instinct, so it can sometimes be difficult to completely eliminate this behaviour.

Solutions

One way to stop your dog from digging is keeping him out of the garden (or whatever location he has selected for this activity) when you cannot watch him. However, if the behaviour is deeply ingrained, he may merely continue digging elsewhere. For this reason, preventing the problem

SENIOR DOG TIP

Patience Is a Virtue

Training an older dog with more entrenched behaviour problems is usually more difficult, but not impossible. Whatever behaviour issue you are trying to correct, you need to act on it as if you were dealing with a younger Shih Tzu. The difference comes in your approach. You must be even more patient and persistent with an older dog. Don't be discouraged by how many previous owners have failed at accomplishing the task. Like people dogs are always learning, and one thing your dog has probably learned is that if he is stubborn enough, people will give up on him. Going just one step further than the last person did can make all the difference!

entirely is a much better option. Increasing the amount of exercise your dog is getting can often head off many problem behaviours such as this, although sometimes a substantial increase will be required before improvement is seen.

If you don't mind letting your dog get a little dirty, but you want to discourage his penchant for digging up your tulips, an alternative way to deal

with the situation might be actually allowing him to dig in his very own spot. Begin by burying a few of his favourite toys in the area you choose, and be sure to let him watch the fun you have in this process. Praise him for digging for his own toys, but redirect him whenever he ventures away from his designated area.

Housesoiling

If your Shih Tzu is repeatedly relieving himself in inappropriate places, remedial housetraining may help. If your dog's feeding and toilleting schedule has become too lax, getting back on track in this area can often solve the problem. If his regression has occurred despite a predictable schedule and consistent effort on your behalf, another problem could be the real issue.

Ruling Out Physical Problems

Your first and best resource is your dog's vet. He or she can help you rule out any underlying medical problems that could be contributing to your dog's inappropriate toiletting. One sign of a urinary tract infection (UTI), for instance, is a strong and frequent urgency to void the bladder. If your dog is suffering from a UTI, simply trying to re-housetrain him will accomplish nothing, and left ignored, his infection will only worsen. Since many serious health conditions present with bladder and bowel-related symptoms, it is imperative that a medical problem is ruled out as soon as possible.

Once your vet has helped you exclude a physiological cause for your Shih Tzu's soiling problem, it is then time to consider other possible reasons for the behaviour. Does your dog spend an excessive amount of time alone? If so, he may not be able to hold his urine or faeces until you get home, or he might be trying to tell you that he needs more attention. Dogs are incredibly intelligent animals, and they have also been known to occasionally hold a grudge or two.

Solutions

If the problem is access to an appropriate elimination spot, you can help your dog by providing him with one of several options. If you cannot make it home during a typical day for a quick walk, consider hiring a dog walker or asking a friend to fill this role. Another alternative is indoor housetraining. Newspapers or a litter tray may not be your first choice, but to most owners either of these is preferable to constant cleanups or ruined carpets and furniture. Just keep in mind that few dogs can toggle between indoor and outdoor training. If you decide to

Paper training may be an option for housesoiling problems.

go the route of the litter tray, your Shih Tzu will likely still need it when you have more free time.

If you suspect that your dog's motives for inappropriate elimination have more to do with loneliness, consider getting a second dog. If your Shih Tzu does best with one-on-one contact with people, consider a professional pet sitter. Both choices offer valuable opportunities for socialisation and exercise for your dog—and just may save your carpet in the process.

Finally, note the times and circumstances of your dog's so-called accidents. This information can yield considerable insight into what he is trying to tell you through his behaviour. Our dogs are always talking to us through their actions; many times all we need to do is listen to them.

Jumping Up

I am someone who doesn't really mind a dog jumping up on me. I have learned from various different canine training authorities, though, that it isn't a good idea to teach this behaviour by tolerating it. Just because I don't mind it, after

FAMILY-FRIENDLY TIP

Establishing Boundaries

If you have children, it is especially important that they understand where the lines for interaction with your Shih Tzu are drawn. Whether your dog is prone to behaviour problems or not, these boundaries should be established as early as possible and adjusted if a crisis emerges. Under normal circumstances even a younger family member may play a role in the training process, but a younger child's distractibility may sabotage your efforts at this crucial stage of training if the designated tasks are too complicated. In the case of aggression, your child could also be seriously hurt if personal space is not respected.

Be careful not to exclude your child from helping altogether. Creating new ways for him or her to participate can help your child avoid feeling left out—or worse, resentful of your Shih Tzu. If your dog is acting aggressively over his food, for example, your child should not be allowed in direct contact with your dog while he is eating. He or she may still be able to help you, however, with measuring out the right amount of food or washing the dishes once your dog has finished his meal. By establishing sensible responsibilities for every family member, you have a much greater chance of correcting your dog's problem, and children can remain involved, but not be placed in jeopardy.

all, doesn't mean that people who visit my home don't mind it. I also frequently take my dogs with me to the park and to my son's sporting events, and there may be people at these places who simply don't like dogs or worse, are afraid of them. For these reasons teaching our dogs not to jump up is important.

Solutions

The best way to avert your Shih Tzu from this behaviour is by teaching the command *down* and consistently reinforcing it. In the past I myself have probably foiled another owner's attempt at properly teaching this technique, as I used to be the first one to say "Oh, that's okay!" whenever a dog would jump up on me. Unfortunately, what I was doing was inadvertently reinforcing the behaviour. Whether our reactions are overly positive or we simply show surprise, if we offer a reaction—any reaction—we are part of the problem. One caveat: If your Shih Tzu's jumping problem is severe or if your dog jumps on someone who is clearly afraid of dogs, you may use a firm, "Off!"

If your dog tends to jump up most often when company first arrives at your home, you can simulate this ritual by having a friend or family member repeatedly "arrive" at your door and enter for a practice session. Keep treats nearby. Before your dog has a chance to jump up, issue the *sit* command. Make sure the "visitor" understands that no reaction should be shown until your dog is sitting. To help ensure

Shih Tzu's love to play, so keep anything you don't want in his mouth off the floor.

that the lesson is learned, try keeping a container of treats by the door, so future guests can utilise this same trick.

Nipping

There are two types of biting, and although one is definitely worse than the other, neither should ever be tolerated. The first is playful biting. While it may sound innocent enough, this form of biting that often resembles chewing usually stems from the teething process, but results in a potentially dangerous habit. Like children, puppies put nearly everything into their mouths, and also like children, puppies need to be provided with appropriate items on which they can chew and ease their teething pain. When owners allow their dogs to chew on their fingers or hands, however, they unintentionally teach them that it is okay to bite

people. Serious aggression problems are rare in well-bred Shih Tzu, but the risk (however small) is multiplied by allowing any biting-like behaviours. By letting your dog bite you—even playfully, you break down the first barrier to a future aggression problem.

Solutions

If your dog starts to use your hand as a teething ring, handle it as you would a chewing issue. Just because his biting doesn't hurt doesn't mean that it is acceptable. And remember, by teaching your dog that he cannot bite you, you essentially teach him that it is wrong to bite other people, as well. Be sure that any other household members comply with your no-biting rule. Children in particular are easy targets for playful biting—and are also at risk of being hurt should the habit escalate down the road.

It is estimated that one in three dogs will be lost at some point in his life. If you and your Shih Tzu are ever separated, it is especially important that you notify the proper authorities as soon as you realise your dog is missing. This will drastically increase your chances of getting him back safe and sound. If your dog has been stolen, this means calling the police and providing them with all pertinent information—a detailed description (including any distinguishing marks), a photograph, and if possible a description of the person who took your Shih Tzu.

If your dog has run away, begin by informing your neighbours of your dog's disappearance as you look for him. If he hasn't had time to venture far, one of them may be able to help you find him by remaining watchful. Next you should get the word out to as many other people as possible. Depending on where you live, this may mean posting flyers wherever you can—lamp-posts, local businesses, everywhere. You should also call your local dog warden, rescue centre, and your dog's vet.

In either of these situations, one of the best ways you can help make sure your dog finds his way back to you is having him microchipped. Without identification, 90-percent of dogs that are lost will not return home. Although the police may locate your Shih Tzu, you will still need to prove ownership. If someone finds your dog and takes him to a veterinary surgery or rescue centre, a microchip will enable these caregivers to reunite you with your beloved dog.

The other, more serious form of biting is angry biting, or aggression. A Shih Tzu displaying aggressive behaviour may be territorial over certain items—his bone or food bowl, for example. This doesn't mean that the dog is hopeless, or even that the dog has an inherently aggressive nature. Remember, aggression may be a natural transition for some dogs from playful biting to more aggressive behaviour when the dog feels threatened. A dog that isn't accustomed to being around children may react aggressively if a child moves too quickly towards him or if the child reaches for his favourite toy. In a situation like this, both the child and the dog can get hurt, so the best thing to do is not allow unsupervised interaction in the first place.

If your Shih Tzu is growling when someone gets too close to his food or belongings, remove the item in question immediately. You may offer it back to him later, making a point of touching the object repeatedly and praising the dog for sharing. If he acts at all intimidating, remove the item again. Repeat this exercise until no aggression is displayed.

If food is the problem, start hand-feeding your dog until he starts behaving better when someone touches his food. A good way to prevent food aggression is by making a point of periodically placing your hand in your dog's dish while he is eating. A child may be allowed to do this in the presence of an adult, but once any aggression has been shown, limit this task to adult caregivers.

Some dogs may bite even when completely unprovoked. If your dog bites you for no apparent reason, you simply must get to the bottom of the problem. Your vet should be able to recommend a trainer or behaviourist in your area that works to resolve this kind of problem. True aggression is a behavioural emergency and needs the attention of a trained professional.

All of your Shih Tzu's interactions with children should be supervised.

Chapter 8

Stepping Out

Certainly one of the advantages of owning a smaller dog is the convenience of being able to take him along with you virtually wherever you go. There is a considerable difference, however, between making a quick jaunt down the street to post a letter or going to pick your kids up from school and venturing halfway across the country. Including your Shih Tzu in your holiday plans doesn't have to be difficult, but it will require some additional planning to make it enjoyable and a safe one for all involved.

Hitting the Road

If you will be travellling by car, making an extended excursion will be much like taking a daytrip with the exception of taking along more of everything you'll need. Taking your Shih Tzu along on your trip is actually a lot like taking a child: preparation is paramount. Make a list of everything you wish to pack and all the things that must be done before leaving. Feed your dog only a light meal prior to the trip—never immediately before leaving the house. This can help prevent stomach upset from travel sickness.

Safety First

Although you may not find it necessary to bring your Shih Tzu's crate along every time you take your dog with

you to run an errand, it really is the most secure place for him while in your vehicle. This is especially true for long-distance journeys that typically involve considerable amounts of time on the motorway. Don't fool yourself into thinking that your dog is safest in your lap. Not only could your Shih Tzu be seriously hurt in the event of an accident (an airbag deployment alone could kill this small breed), but also he could actually cause a collision by simply being a dog and distracting the driver.

Dealing With Carsickness

If your dog is prone to carsickness, do the same thing you would do for a human passenger—open a window. Unlike people, though, dogs cannot use words to tell you when they start feeling queasy. Signs that your Shih Tzu may be carsick include yawning or excessive drooling, often followed by vomiting. Fresh air can often head off a nausea attack, as can positioning your dog's crate so he can see out of a window. If your dog often experiences intense symptoms, ask your vet about giving him travel sickness medication prior to your trip.

The Air Up There

In the UK, we rarely need to travel abroad with our dogs. But with the Pet Passport Scheme (PETS), foreign travel, including air travel, is becoming an increasingly popular option.

Requesting a list of your airline's rules and regulations for canine travel can make flying easier on both you and your dog. Complete this task as soon as you begin planning your holiday, so you will have enough time to get any paperwork (such as health certificates) or veterinary visits (for rabies vaccinations) out of the way well before your trip.

Air Travel Safety

Flying during hot weather can be difficult for dogs, since the heat in the cargo areas at these times can be severe. When evaluating the temperature, consider the climate not only where you live, but where you will be going, as well. Scheduling your flight for early morning or late evening can reduce your dog's risk of overheating, but some airlines have strict policies of not transporting

FAMILY-FRIENDLY TIP

"Are We There Yet?"

Travelling with either a dog or a child can be stressful, but there are some things you can do make your excursion a pleasant one for you, your kids, and your Shih Tzu. First, make sure everyone is safely secured before pulling out of the driveway. You wouldn't leave without your two-year-old safely buckled into a carseat, right? So why should you allow your beloved Shih Tzu to roam around the vehicle as you cruise along the motorway? The safest place for your pup is in a crate, preferably belted into place. Taking this easy step also helps ensure that any small children are also kept safe from bites or scratches while you are driving.

Parents may think to take along books and small toys for their kids, but what about similar amusements for your dog? If your Shih Tzu has a favourite chew toy, this may be ideal for making the journey seem shorter for him, as well. It can also serve as an item of comfort during scary moments if your dog is new to travelling.

Finally, remember that both kids and dogs need frequent breaks when travelling long distances. Unless it will take several hours to reach your destination, it is best to hold off on meals until you arrive. It is a good idea, though, to give both kids and dogs regular breaks to stretch their legs, drink some water, and relieve their bladders. And like your mother always told you, don't forget to *go* before leaving the house!

What to Pack

When my son was younger, I never left the house without a mammoth bag stuffed with anything (and everything) we'd possibly need. When travelling with my dogs, I find that this same bag still comes in quite handy. I'm just filling it with different things now. Instead of animal crackers, I pack dog treats. In place of a rattle, I stash a squeak toy. And of course, I bring along cleanup bags instead of nappies.

When you will be away for more than an afternoon, however, you will need to pack a few more things. In addition to food and water, your dog will need bowls. Collapsible bowls are small enough to store in a handbag or glovebox until needed. Some owners find a thermos a more useful choice, as it can store food or water *and* provide a drinking bowl.

Your dog's crate is not only a safe place for him to travel, but it also provides him with an ideal spot to eat or rest once you arrive at your destination. Remember to bring along a padded liner or a blanket to use as a cushion.

One of the most versatile items you can pack is a box of zip-style plastic bags. By rolling down the sides, these become wonderful impromptu water bowls. They can also be used for holding various belongings, or serve as cleanup bags when necessary.

An item I decided would remain in my original bag of tricks is a container of baby wipes. Handy for all kinds of cleanups, I have used these on nearly every trip I have taken with my dogs.

animals during warmer months. Although smaller dogs are sometimes permitted to ride in the plane's cabin with their owners, there is usually a limited number of dogs allowed on a single flight, so don't assume that your Shih Tzu will be able to travel with you.

If your dog will be travelling in the cargo area, I strongly recommend investing in a bungie cord. In the event of an emergency, your dog should always be quickly accessible, so locking your Shih Tzu's crate door is not a practical option. Securing the crate with a bungie cord, however, is a good way to protect your pet from getting hurt should his door pop open unexpectedly at any time during the trip.

Regardless of where your dog will be during the flight, try to book seats at the front of the plane, so you are among the first passengers off to exit once you reach your destination. This is especially important if you will be catching a connecting flight. Even better, book a direct flight whenever possible.

Chateau Shih Tzu—Finding Dog-friendly Lodging

Bringing your Shih Tzu with you on holiday without calling ahead to make sure that your dog is welcome at the hotel of your choice can land both of you out in the cold. Many quality establishments are finally realising that people want their faithful companions to join them on holiday, and more and more businesses are allowing canine guests to check in along with their owners.

Whether you're planning a weekend ski trip, a family holiday to a thrilling amusement park, or you're looking for a cottage on the lake for a month-long stay, you need to find pet-friendly accommodation. Obviously you can check with staff to find out if your Shih Tzu is welcome. But it is much easier to plan your trip around pet-friendly establishments. You can get relevant information by logging on to www. petfriendly.co.uk for pet-friendly hotels in the UK or www.preferredplaces.co.uk, which lists holiday cottages where pets are welcome. For a website that gives details of pet-friendly hotels, cottages and camping, try www.dogsinvited.co.uk.

Showing Your Shih Tzu

Dog shows (often called conformation events) began as a way of evaluating breeding stock. For this reason only purebred dogs that have not yet been spayed or neutered are eligible to compete as a show dog. Dogs must also be at least six months old. Although many owners think their Shih Tzu are perfect, show dogs must meet extremely demanding criteria for both physical qualities and temperament. Imperfections an owner might never even notice about a dog—a slightly overshot bite, for example, are often considered serious faults in conformation. Only Shih Tzu that most closely match the dog's breed standard, the official description of an ideal Shih Tzu, have a realistic chance of winning in the ring.

Show dogs must meet extremely demanding criteria for both physical qualities and temperament.

BEST OF
OPPOSITE SEX

Shih Tzu

SENIOR DOG TIP

No Accidental Tourist

The best way to ensure that your older dog handles travelling well is by introducing him to the process as soon as possible. Puppies that are used to crates, car rides, and strangers will tolerate these things considerably better as adults than animals never before exposed to the often hectic and sometimes scary world of travel. A great way to *travel-train* your dog at any age is taking him for shorter trips more often, gradually lengthening the duration of these outings, and praising him every step (or mile) along the way. If your Shih Tzu has already entered his golden years, you may need to take a few additional steps to make your joint holiday more comfortable for him. This may be as simple as furnishing his crate with a little extra padding (especially if your dog is arthritic), or it may mean making more frequent pit stops for him to stretch his arthritic legs and relieve his ageing bladder.

A Shih Tzu may be entered in a multi-breed show where he will be included as a member of the utility group, or he may participate in a breed show, an event involving just a single breed.

For a dog to become a Champion, he or she must win a Challenge Certificate (CC) under three different judges. These dogs have the right to use the title Champion (or Ch.) before their names.

If you are interested in showing your Shih Tzu, the best way to learn about this exciting activity is by attending a conformation event as a spectator. One thing I have learned from doing so is that most breeders and handlers love meeting other people who are smitten with their breed. Most will freely offer you tips on how to get involved in showing or how to find a dog well suited to the ring. Be considerate enough to wait to approach these people until they are done showing their dogs, though, as *show time* can be a very hectic occasion.

Sports and Other Activities

Agility

If your Shih Tzu has a penchant for playtime, agility may be a fun activity the two of your can share. Requiring speed and dexterity, agility competitions offer dogs a chance to show off their physical prowess. Resembling an equestrian jumping competition, the setting for agility consists of a variety of colourful jumps, vaulted walks, see-saws, A-frames, and tunnels. Handlers lead their dogs through the course by running alongside them and offering either verbal commands or hand signals (or both) as the dogs navigate these obstacles.

Agility can be as fun for spectators as it is for participants, and the sport regularly draws impressive crowds. Developed in England in the 1970s, it was first recognised by the AKC in 1994. Unlike the requirements for conformation, a dog need not be purebred to compete in agility, and entrants may also be spayed or neutered. The one requirement that is more stringent, however, is a minimum age of 12 months for all canine participants.

In Agility competitions, competitors start at Elementary level and work their way up through Starters, Novice, and Intermediate, to Advanced. Not everyone who participates pursues all of these levels, however, or

competes in every competition. The best thing about agility is that it is something you can do with your Shih Tzu right in your own garden. You need not ever enter a formal competition to participate, though it might be a whole lot of fun!

Obedience

Just as some dogs seem destined for conformation or agility, some are amazingly well suited to obedience training. You may notice this when training your dog at home, or this may be your goal from the beginning. Although all breeds (and mixed breeds) are welcome to participate in obedience, the small breeds are few and far between. It is a world dominated by Border Collies. However, your Shih Tzu is in no way less capable of excelling at obedience, so if you have an interest in this activity, run with it, remembering to heel when appropriate, of course.

Unlike the sport of agility, which focuses on a dog's physical abilities and allows considerable owner interaction, obedience requires more discipline than athleticism; it is truly a test of how well your

101

Agility may be a fun activity the two of you can share.

Sports and Safety

You've heard the standard warning: *Before beginning an exercise programme, consult your doctor.* **This is excellent advice, not only for people, but for dogs, as well. Especially if your Shih Tzu is older or overweight, you should discuss any physical activities you are considering for him with your vet, so you can be sure he is in proper shape to meet the demands of the sport.**

dog can do on his own. Among the commands your Shih Tzu will be required to perform at the basic level of competitive obedience are heeling (both on and off his lead), sitting and staying for several minutes at a time, and also standing and staying for similarly fixed time periods. Certainly, owners are involved in every aspect of training (and this is no small task), and they are allowed to issue the commands, but you won't find these owners cheering until the day is done.

Dogs begin competing in the Pre-beginners class and then move on to Beginners, Novice, Class A, Class B and Class C. The highest award is to become an Obedience Champion, which means winning in Class C and being awarded a Challenge Certificate under three different judges.

Games

Playing games with your Shih Tzu is an excellent way of providing him with essential physical exercise and mental stimulation. It can also offer you both a much-needed break from the more serious side of life. If there's one thing that dogs seem to innately understand that we humans don't, it's the value of unabashed fun. They don't worry about making fools of themselves, they don't need any fancy equipment, and perhaps most importantly, they don't put off playtime in favour of a higher priority or for when they will have more time. To your Shih Tzu, just a few minutes is more than enough time for whatever game he enjoys most.

In addition to the more traditional canine games such as fetch and squeak

Lord of the Dance

My own dogs love dancing. There is just something about music that makes people want to move, and dogs can certainly share in this amusing activity. Dancing is also great exercise, so get those cd's spinning, start moving, and even sing along if you like. Your Shih Tzu will likely join you in bopping around the house, and he'll never tell anyone how silly you look.

You may find that your dog enjoys many of the same games that you and your kids do.

the plastic newspaper, you can easily invent your own games to play with your dog. They need not be intricate—many won't even require any props.

You may also find that your dog enjoys many of the same games that you and your kids do. A tetherball pole in the garden, for instance, can be extremely fun. Although your Shih Tzu is allowed to jump up and bat the ball with any of his paws as hard as he likes, the rules must be that you only use your hands (no kicking whatsoever) and very lightly so.

Other fun games for your dog may include follow the leader or hide and seek. For the former activity, you can get down on all fours and do things your dog can easily imitate—like stomping, barking, lying on your back, and rolling over. For hide and seek, always make sure you are the one hiding, as you should never teach your dog to run away or hide from you. Teaching him to seek you out, on the other hand, can be an excellent means of reinforcing the *come* command.

Resources

Associations and Organisations

Breed Clubs

American Kennel Club (AKC)
5580 Centerview Drive
Raleigh, NC 27606
Telephone: (919) 233-9767
Fax: (919) 233-3627
E-mail: info@akc.org
www.akc.org

Canadian Kennel Club (CKC)
89 Skyway Avenue, Suite 100
Etobicoke, Ontario M9W 6R4
Telephone: 416 675 5511
Fax: 416 675 6506
E-mail: information@ckc.ca
www.ckc.ca

Federation Cynologique Internationale (FCI)
Secretariat General de la FCI
Place Albert 1er,
13B – 6530 Thuin
Belqique
www.fci.be

The Kennel Club
1 Clarges Street
LondonW1J 8AB
Telephone: 0870 606 6750
Fax: 0207 518 1058
www.the-kennel-club.org.uk

The Shih Tzu Club
Secretary: Mrs. Pat Gregory
Marpalyn, 5 Radnor Park
Corston, Malmesbury
Wiltshire SN16 0HE

Telephone: 01666 82238
E-mail: secretary@theshihtzuclub.co.uk
http://www.theshihtzuclub.co.uk

The Shih Tzu Club of Scotland
Secretary: Mr Martin
Telephone: 01414 240160

The Shih Tzu Club of Wales and Western Counties
Secretary: Miss W Rewbury
Telephone: 01823 33586

United Kennel Club (UKC)
100 E. Kilgore Road
Kalamazoo, MI 49002-5584
Telephone: 269 343 9020
Fax: 269 343 7037
E-mail: pbickell@ukcdogs.com
www.ukcdogs.com

Pet Sitters

National Association of Registered Petsitters
www.dogsit.com

UK Petsitters
Telephone: 01902 41789
www.ukpetsitter.com

Dog Services UK
www.dogservices.co.uk

104

Shih Tzu

Rescue Organisations and Animal Welfare Groups

British Veterinary AssociationAnimal Welfare Foundation (BVA AWF)
7 Mansfield Street
London W1G 9NQ
Telephone: 0207 636 6541
Fax: 0207 436 2970
Email: bva-awf@bva.co.uk
www.bva-awf.org.uk/about

Royal Society for the Prevention of Cruelty to Animals (RSPCA)
Telephone: 0870 3335 999
Fax: 0870 7530 284
www.rspca.org.uk

Scottish Society for the Prevention of Cruelty to Animals (SSPCA)
Braehead Mains,
603 Queensferry Road
Edinburgh EH4 6EA
Telephone: 0131 339 0222
Fax: 0131 339 4777
Email: enquiries@scottishspca.org
www.scottishspca.org/about

Sports

Agility Club UK
www.agilityclub.co.uk

British Flyball Association
PO Box 109
Petersfield GU32 1XZ
Telephone: 01753 620110
Fax: 01726 861079
Email: bfa@flyball.org.uk
www.flyball.org.uk

Canine Freestyle Federation, Inc.
Secretary: Brandy ClymireE-Mail: secretary@canine-freestyle.org
www.canine-freestyle.org

International Agility Link (IAL)
Global Administrator: Steve DrinkwaterE-mail: yunde@powerup.auwww.agilityclick.com/~ial

World Canine Freestyle Organisation
P.O. Box 350122Brooklyn, NY 11235-2525Telephone: (718) 332-8336www.worldcannefreestyle.org

Therapy

Pets As Therapy
3 Grange Farm Cottages
Wycombe Road, Saunderton
Princes Risborough
Bucks HP27 9NS
Telephone: 0870 977 0003
Fax: 0870 706 2562
www.petsastherapy.org

Therapy Dogs International (TDI)
88 Bartley Road
Flanders, NJ 07836
Telephone: (973) 252-9800
Fax: (973) 252-7171
E-mail: tdi@gti.net
www.tdi-dog.org

Training and Behaviour

Association of Pet Dog Trainers (APDT)
PO Box 17
Kempsford GL7 4W7
Telephone: 01285 810811

Association of Pet Behaviour Counsellors
PO Box 46
Worcester WR8 9YS
Telephone: 01386 751151
Fax: 01386 750743
Email: info@apbc.org.uk
www.apbc.org.uk

Veterinary and Health Resources

American Veterinary Medical Association (AVMA)
1931 North Meacham Road – Suite 100
Schaumburg, IL 60173
Telephone: 847 925-8070
Fax: 847 925 1329
E-mail: avmainfo@avma.org
www.avma.org

Association of British Veterinary Acupuncturists (ABVA)
66A Easthorpe, Southwell
Nottinghamshire NG25 0HZ
Email: jonnyboyvet@hotmail.com
www.abva.co.uk

Association of Chartered Physiotherapists Specialising in
Animal Therapy (ACPAT)
52 Littleham Road
Exmoouth, Devon EX8 2QJ
Telephone/Fax: 01395 270648
Email: bexsharples@hotmail.com
www.acpat.org.uk

British Association of Homoeopathic Veterinary Surgeons
Alternative Veterinary
Medicine Centre
Chinham House

Stanford in the Vale
Oxfordshire SN7 8NQ
Email: enquiries@bahvs.com
www.bahvs.com

British Association of Veterinary Opthalmologists (BAVO)
Email: hjf@vetspecialists.co.uk
Email: secretary@bravo.org.uk
www.bravo.oprg.uk

British Small Animal Veterinary Association (BSAVA)
Woodrow House, 1 Telford Way
Waterwells Business Park
Quedgley, Gloucester GL2 2AB
Telephone: 01452 726700
Fax: 01452 726701
Email: customerservices@bsava.com
www.bsava.com

British Veterinary Association (BVA)
7 Mansfield Street
LondonW1G 9NQ
Telephone: 020 7636 6541
Fax: 020 7436 2970
E-mail: bvahq@bva.co.uk
www.bva.co.uk

British Veterinary Hospitals Association (BHVA)
Station Bungalow
Main Road, Stockfield
Northumberland NE43 7HJ
Telephone: 07966 901619
Fax: 07813 915954
Email: office@bvha.org.uk
www.BVHA.org.uk

Royal College of Veterinary
Surgeons (RCVS)
Belgravia House, 62-64 Horseferry Road
London SW1P 2AF
Telephone: 0207 222 2001
Email: admin@rcvs.org.uk
www.rcvs.org.uk

Publications

Newspapers and Magazines

Dog World Ltd
Somerfield House
Wotton Road, Ashford
Kent TN23 6LW
Telephone: 01233 621877

Dogs Monthly
Ascot House, High Street,
Ascot, Berkshire SL5 7JG
Telephone: 0870 730 8433
E-mail: admin@rtc-associates.freeserve.co.uk
www.corsini.co.uk/dogsmonthly

Dogs Today
Town Mill, Bagshot Road
Chobham, Surrey GU24 8BZ
Telephone: 01276 858880
Email: enquiries@dogstodaymagazine.co.uk
www.dogstodaymagazine.co.uk

Kennel Gazette
Kennel Club
1 Clarges Street, London W1J 8AB
Telephone: 0870 606 6750
www.the-kennel-club.co.uk

K9 Magazine
21 High Street
Warsop, Nottinghamshire NG20 0AA
Telephone: 0870 011 4114

Email: mail@k9magazine.com
www.k9magazine.com

Our Dogs
Our Dogs Publishing
5 Oxford Road
Station Approach
Manchester M60 1SX
www.ourdogs.co.uk

Your Dog
Roebuck House
33 Broad Street, Stamford
Lincolnshire PE9 1RB
Telephone: 01780 766199

Books
The Super Simple Guide to
Housetraining
Anderson, Teoti.
Neptune, NJ: TFH Publications, 2004.

Good Dogkeeping
Morgan, Diane.
Neptune, NJ: TFH Publications, 2005.

How to Behave So Your Dog Behaves
Yin, Sophia, DVM
Neptune, NJ: TFH Publications, 2004.

The Mini Encyclopedia of Dog Training
& Behaviour
Tennant, Colin
Dorking, Surrey: Interpet Publishing,
2005

What If My Dog...?
Evans, Jim
Dorking, Surrey, Interpet Publishing,
2006

Index

Index

Index

Dedication

To the memory of my grandmother, Dorothy Perkins, and to my grandfather, Malcolm Perkins—who together nurtured by love for animals by buying me my very first dog. And to the memory of their beloved Shih Tzu, Tammy, my namesake.

Acknowledgements

The author would like to thank the following people for sharing their valuable experiences and insights with the author: Sherry Bolinger, Breeder; Daryl Conner, Professional Dog Groomer; Karen Coutu, Breeder; Dr. Monica Diedrich, Animal Communicator; Donna Foss, Breeder; Margaret O'Brennan, Owner; Diane Ramm, Breeder; Kathy Slifka, Breeder; Krystal Thompson, Owner; Debbie Wong, Owner.

About the Author

Tammy Gagne is a freelance writer who specialises in the health and behaviour of companion animals. She is a regular contributor to several American pet care magazines and has owned purebred dogs for more than 25 years. In addition to being an avid dog lover, she is also an experienced aviculturist and writes a bi-monthly column that appears in *Bird Times* magazine. She resides in northern New England with her husband, son, dogs, and parrots.